SEO Isn't Magic—It's Just Strategy (Done Right)

Let's clear something up: SEO isn't some mysterious dark art or reserved only for nerds in basements. It's not about tricking algorithms or stuffing keywords like it's 2006. It's a skill—one that, when done right, can make or break your business.

The problem? Most people either don't understand it—or worse, think they do. They follow outdated advice, buy backlinks from Fiverr, or install one plugin and call it a day. And don't even get me started on people who think five lines of Organizational schema is enough. That's not SEO. That's checkbox marketing.

This book is here to fix that.

My Story (and Why You Should Even Care)

I've been obsessed with the internet since I was a kid. Like, really obsessed. I was six when we got our first computer—one of those noisy, clunky ones that made you feel like a hacker just for opening Minesweeper. And so it all started with games.

At eleven, I was spending my precious one hour a day online customizing LiveJournal-like profiles and figuring out how some posts magically ranked in Google. By thirteen, I was running forums and building pages that ranked—without even knowing what SEO was.

By fourteen, I was building websites for friends, family, random side hustles—sushi delivery, mobile car washes, you name it. Through trial and error (and way too many all-nighters), I learned what actually made websites work.

Then came my first proper job in marketing, a move to the UK, and seven years of professional deep-diving into eCommerce and SEO. I worked with big companies, small shops, and chaotic founders who needed results *yesterday*. I learned how to grow traffic fast—and how to do it without burning budget or relying on gurus selling dreams.

Eventually, I hit a wall. Same companies. Same problems. Same politics. So, I did what any restless, slightly rebellious marketer does: I started my own agency—Ace It SEO. Now, I work with businesses I *choose*, using strategies that *actually work*, not whatever's trending this week.

Why This Book Exists

I've read most of the "top-rated" SEO books out there. Some are okay. Most are outdated, too theoretical, or straight-up wrong. None of them cover everything. And the ones that do? They either bore you to death or cost £2,000 in course format.

This book is different. It's structured like a proper learning path—start to finish. It's practical. You'll have tasks, real exercises, tools, and examples you can copy, tweak, or build on. By the end, you'll not only understand SEO—you'll *own* it.

Whether you're a business owner tired of paying for overpriced SEO "specialists" with zero results, or someone who wants to learn SEO as a career path—this is your manual. No fluff. No fake hacks. Just strategies that work in 2025 and beyond.

What You'll Learn (Without Losing Your Mind)

We're starting from scratch: how search engines think, how to build your first keyword list, how to fix technical issues without a dev team. Then we'll move into more advanced stuff: schema, link building, voice search, AI content, you name it.

I'll walk you through everything step by step—with real examples, checklists, and bite-sized action items after each chapter.

You'll learn:

- What Google actually wants (spoiler: not keyword stuffing)
- How to make content that ranks *and* converts
- How to build links the right way—without begging or paying
- What tools are worth your time (and which are all hype)
- How to diagnose traffic drops like a pro
- And how to avoid the classic mistakes that cost businesses thousands

Oh—and I'll bust some SEO myths while we're at it. Like the idea that "basic schema is enough." It's not. You're leaving money, clicks, and visibility on the table if you're not using every field that makes sense for your site.

Who This Book Is For

- Website owners who want more traffic (and sales) without hiring an agency

- Freelancers or marketers who want to level up their SEO game
- Business owners who've been burned by bad SEO before
- Anyone tired of vague advice and ready for actual strategy

This isn't a quick fix. It's not "rank #1 in 5 days." It's a playbook. Read it, apply it, tweak it, repeat. SEO is a long game—but if you do it right, the results last. Let's get to work.

Chapter 1: What Is SEO and How Does It Work?

SEO, In Plain English

Let's cut the jargon. SEO—Search Engine Optimization—isn't magic, and it's definitely not about "hacking" Google. At its core, SEO is just this: the art and science of getting your website to appear when someone searches for what you offer.

Think about the last time you searched for something like:

- *"Best beginner-friendly DSLR cameras under $500"*
- *"Sourdough bread recipe without starter"*
- *"Furniture store near me"*

Those weren't just idle searches. You had intent—a goal, a curiosity, or a problem to solve. SEO is how businesses and creators meet that intent by showing up at the right moment with the right content.

So, forget the myths. You don't need to be a developer. You don't need to be a marketing guru. What you do need is to understand three things:

1. How search engines work
2. What your audience wants

3. How to align your website with both

Master those, and you win traffic. And not just *any* traffic—the kind that converts.

How Google Actually Works: Behind the Scenes

Let's lift the hood on what search engines actually do. Google doesn't just magically know which site to show you. It relies on a step-by-step process:

1. **Crawling** – Discovering Your Site

Think of Google like a curious spider weaving its web across the internet. Its "crawlers" or "bots" scan every website they can find, hopping from link to link like a digital librarian scanning book titles. This process is called crawling.

If your site is hard to navigate, has broken pages, or tells bots to go away with a misconfigured robots.txt, Google might not see it at all.

 If Google can't crawl your page, it can't index or rank it. Period.

2. **Indexing** – Storing the Content

Once Google crawls your page, it decides whether to store it in its massive, ever-evolving index. Think of the index as Google's library. Your page becomes a "book" on a shelf, waiting to be discovered.

But here's the kicker: just being on the shelf doesn't mean you'll be recommended. You need to give Google a reason to pull your page out when someone types in a search.

3. **Ranking** – Deciding What Shows Up

This is the money step. When someone enters a query—like *"how to fix a leaky faucet"*—Google scours its indexed pages to find the most relevant, helpful, and trustworthy results.

This is where SEO shines. It's your job to make your content:

- Helpful (solves a problem)
- Relevant (matches the query)
- Trustworthy (credible and up to date)

Google doesn't always favor the biggest brand. It favors the best answer.

What Google Really Wants

Google's goal isn't just to rank websites. Its mission is to organize the world's information and deliver the most relevant, high-quality result for any search.

To do that, it evaluates content using three big questions:

- Relevance: Does this content match the user's intent?
- Quality: Is it well-written, complete, and updated?
- Trust: Can this source be believed?

Let's say someone Googles *"how to clean suede shoes."*

Google's ideal top result would include:

- Step-by-step cleaning instructions
- Recommended tools or products
- Visuals (photos or a quick video)
- A short FAQ for common shoe care questions

It's not looking for a 300-word keyword-stuffed blog post. It's looking for useful content.

The Role of Keywords – Still Critical (Just Smarter Now)

Keywords are still the foundation of SEO—but the way we use them has changed.

Old SEO:

- Stuff the exact keyword 15 times
- Ignore readability or intent

Modern SEO:

- Understand *why* people search
- Use related terms and synonyms
- Answer questions fully

Don't just think "What keyword?" Think: "What problem is this person trying to solve?"

Types of Search Intent (This Is HUGE)

Let's break down intent, which is the secret sauce of great SEO. There are three main types of search intent:

1. Informational

They want to *learn something*

- "What is SEO?"
- "How to make sourdough starter"

Content to use: Blog posts, guides, tutorials

2. **Navigational**

They want to *go to a specific brand or site*

- "Spotify login"
- "Nike running shoes"

Content to use: Branded landing pages or homepage

3. **Transactional**

They're *ready to act*—buy, book, download

- "Best gaming chair under $200"
- "Buy standing desk UK"

Content to use: Product pages, landing pages, service pages

If you're unsure what kind of content
Google expects for a keyword, just
Google it. Look at the top 5 results.
Are they blog posts? Product pages?
Video tutorials? That's your roadmap.

Why SEO Still Matters (Even in a TikTok World)

With social media everywhere and algorithms constantly shifting, you might wonder if SEO is still worth it.

Short answer? Absolutely.

Here's why:

- Searchers are intentional. Unlike social media where you interrupt people, SEO lets you show up *when they're already looking.*
- It's durable. A blog post or product page can bring in traffic for *years.* Ads stop the moment you stop paying.
- It converts. Organic traffic tends to have higher purchase or signup intent than social or paid.

SEO is like owning land. Ads are renting space. The longer you invest in SEO, the more it pays off.

Common SEO Myths (Let's Bust These Now)

There's still a lot of misinformation out there. Let's tackle a few common myths:

Myth #1: SEO is just about ranking #1
Truth: It's about ranking for the *right* keywords—ones that actually convert.

Myth #2: SEO is about "tricking" Google
Truth: It's about *helping* Google understand your value.

Myth #3: You can "set and forget" SEO
Truth: SEO evolves. Google updates regularly. Your content and site should too.

Myth #4: Install an SEO plugin = Done
Truth: Tools help. But strategy, content, and structure win the game.

A Real-World SEO Snapshot: The Bradford Bakery

Let's say you run a local bakery in Bradford and want more people to find you online.

What can you do?

- Add your business to Google Business Profile
- Optimize your homepage for "artisan bakery in Bradford"
- Write blogs like "Best Birthday Cakes in Bradford" or "How to Store Fresh Sourdough"
- Get listed on local directories and foodie blogs

Suddenly, instead of hoping for foot traffic, you're being *found* by people who are already hungry and searching.

That's SEO in action.

Quick Action Exercise: Spy on Google Like a Pro

Want to see how this works in the real world?

Step 1: Think of something you searched recently—*"best yoga mat for beginners"* for example.

Step 2: Google it again. But this time, analyze the results.

Ask yourself:

- What kind of content is showing up?
- What headlines and meta descriptions are being used?
- Are the answers actually helpful?
- How could you create something even better?

Jot your notes down—you'll build your keyword and content strategy on insights like these.

Coming Up Next:
Now that you understand what SEO is and how it works, we're going to lay the groundwork. In the next section, we'll talk about setting your website up for SEO success—before you write a single blog or optimize a single product page.

Because if your site is slow, broken, or confusing... even the best content won't save you.

Chapter 2: Setting Up Your Website for SEO Success

Before you write a single word of content, your site needs a solid foundation.

SEO Starts *Before* Content

Most people jump into SEO by writing blog posts or obsessing over keywords. But that's like decorating a house before you've poured the concrete. If the foundation is weak—slow load speeds, broken links, messy URLs—no amount of content can make up for it.

This chapter is your blueprint for building an SEO-ready website. From your domain name to your mobile responsiveness, every decision here affects whether Google will *see* and *trust* your site—or ignore it altogether.

1. Choosing the Right Domain Name and Hosting

Your domain is your digital storefront. It should be simple, memorable, and aligned with your brand—not just crammed with keywords.

Domain Name Best Practices:

- Short and readable: Aim for clarity over cleverness.
- Avoid hyphens, numbers, or odd spellings: These make it hard to remember and harder to share.
- Use relevant TLDs: If you're UK-based, .co.uk works well. If you're global, .com is still the gold standard.

Example:

- www.best-cheap-furniture-uk-online-store.biz →

  confusing and spammy

- www.cheapfurniturewarehouse.co.uk → clear and

  trustable

Your domain should look trustworthy at a glance—especially on mobile.

Hosting: Don't Skimp

Hosting is often treated as an afterthought—but it's one of the biggest SEO levers. A fast, reliable host improves:

- Page load times
- Site uptime
- Google's perception of your site's stability

Choose a host that offers:

- Fast performance (low TTFB)
- Servers near your main audience or support for a CDN (Content Delivery Network)
- Staging environments for safe testing

If your hosting frequently crashes, no
SEO strategy will save you.

2. Website Structure – Clean, Clear, Crawlable

Think of your site's structure as its internal map. It guides users and search engines alike. If pages are buried, disconnected, or disorganized, Google won't see them—and visitors won't trust you.

Essentials of a Good Site Structure:

- Use readable URLs (spot the best option)
  - /products/oak-dining-table
  - /product?id=987654321
- Keep it flat
  - Most content should be accessible within 2–3 clicks from the homepage.
- Use logical categories
  - For eCommerce or blogs:
    - /blog/seo/technical-seo-basics
    - /furniture/bedroom/wooden-beds
- Keep the main menu simple
  - Avoid clutter—prioritize key categories and make navigation intuitive.

Would a first-time visitor instantly understand where to go next?

3. Essential Tools to Install on Day One

If SEO is about making smart decisions, you need data—and that means setting up analytics and monitoring tools right from the start.

Here's your starter stack:

Google Analytics 4

Tracks user behavior, traffic sources, engagement, and conversions. Even if you're not ready to analyze, install it so you start collecting data.

Google Search Console

Google's direct line to you. It shows:

- What keywords bring users to your site

- How your site appears in search results
- Crawl errors and mobile issues
- Indexing status of your pages

Use it to:

- Submit sitemaps
- Monitor performance
- Fix crawl or indexing issues
- Get real-time alerts when something goes wrong

Bing Webmaster Tools

Yes, Bing is still a thing—and its insights can be surprisingly valuable, especially for older demographics or B2B audiences. Another thing I unexpectedly loved about Bing is that it crawls backlinks way faster than Google—gives you a chance to spot spammy backlinks and disavow them in time.

Optional (But Highly Recommended) Tools:

- Hotjar / Microsoft Clarity – Visual heatmaps and session recordings.
- Screaming Frog (free up to 500 URLs) – Find broken links, duplicate titles, and technical issues.

- Ahrefs Webmaster Tools – Offers SEO health audits even on the free tier.

 Install these tools before launching your first blog post. Every day without data is a missed opportunity to learn.

4. Set Up Your Sitemap and Robots.txt

Sitemap: Your Site's GPS for Google

A sitemap tells search engines:

- What pages exist
- Which ones are important
- When they were last updated

Most CMS platforms (WordPress, Webflow, Shopify) generate this automatically.

Steps:

1. Locate your sitemap: usually at yourdomain.com/sitemap.xml
2. Submit it in Google Search Console > Sitemaps
3. Done

Bonus: Clean sitemaps also help you catch indexing problems early.

Robots.txt: Managing Crawl Access

This file controls what parts of your site Googlebot can and can't visit.

Sample robots.txt

```
User-agent: *
Disallow: /cart/
Disallow: /checkout/
```

Don't overblock! Accidentally disallowing / (your whole site) will prevent Google from seeing *anything*.

5. Secure Your Site with HTTPS

Google has made it crystal clear: security matters.

Sites without HTTPS:

- Trigger browser warnings
- Lose user trust instantly
- Suffer lower rankings

To secure your site:

- Get an SSL certificate (usually free via your host)
- Set up redirects from all HTTP versions to HTTPS
- Check for duplicates (www vs non-www, http vs https)

Tool: Use an HTTP-to-HTTPS redirect checker to confirm only one version of your domain loads.

Coming Up Next

You've now laid the technical foundation of your site. In the next page, we'll cover mobile responsiveness, trust-building content, and a hands-on checklist to run your very first full SEO health check.

Chapter 3: Keyword Research – The Heart of SEO

If SEO is a car, keywords are the fuel. Get this wrong, and you're going nowhere fast.

Why Keyword Research Matters More Than Ever

Let's get something straight: keywords are not dead—they've just grown up.

In the early days of SEO, you could toss a few high-volume phrases into a page and rank overnight. That era is long gone. Today, keyword research isn't about stuffing search terms into content. It's about understanding *how people think, what they want, and how close they are to taking action.*

Think of keyword research as eavesdropping on your market. You're listening in on what real people are typing into search bars—when they're curious, confused, comparing, or ready to buy.

If you know what your audience is searching for—and why— they'll land on *your* site instead of your competitor's. And they'll stay.

The Biggest Mistake: Chasing Volume, Ignoring Intent

Here's a common trap: people pick keywords with 10,000+ searches per month and think they've struck gold.

But search volume alone doesn't mean the keyword will bring you traffic that converts. What really matters is intent—what the person behind that search is actually trying to do.

Let's break down intent into three categories:

1. **Informational Intent**

The user is looking to learn.

- "What is SEO?"
- "How to grow succulents indoors"
- "Why is my Wi-Fi so slow?"

These searchers want guides, tutorials, or blog posts. If you give them clarity, you build trust—and earn the chance to convert them later.

2. **Navigational Intent**

The user wants to find a specific site or brand.

- "Notion templates"
- "Nike shoes men's"

- "Mailchimp login"

These keywords work best when you own the brand or are targeting a branded category. They're not for general content play.

3. **Transactional** (a.k.a. Commercial) **Intent**

The user is ready to take action—buy, sign up, download, or contact.

- "Best CRM for small business"
- "Buy standing desk UK"
- "Affordable logo design service"

These are high-intent, high-value searches. If you have the right product or service page in place, they can be SEO gold.

Which Intent Should You Target?

All three—at different stages.

A solid SEO strategy attracts people:

- Before they're ready to buy (with helpful content),
- When they're comparing options (with guides and reviews),

- And when they're ready to take action (with optimized landing pages).

Start with a few transactional keywords if you need quick wins. Then build a content moat with informational topics.

Short-Tail vs. Long-Tail Keywords: What Really Matters

Forget the myth that short-tail (broad) keywords are the "big leagues." They're often too vague, too competitive and too risky for smaller or new sites. Too many 'too'.

Let's compare:

Short-Tail Keyword: "headphones"

- Huge volume, high competition
- Intent is unclear: are they buying? Comparing? Learning?

Long-Tail Keyword: "best noise-cancelling headphones under £200"

- Lower volume, *way* more specific
- Clear purchase intent

Rule of thumb: Long-tail keywords attract *fewer* visitors—but they're *more likely to convert.*

Where to Find Great Keywords (Without Paying for 10 Tools)

Let's keep this practical. You don't need a full agency tech stack to find great keywords. Start with these core methods:

1. **Google's Own Search Bar**

Start typing a topic and see what Google auto-suggests. That's *real user data.*

Example: Type "how to clean suede" →

You'll see:

- "how to clean suede without vinegar"
- "how to clean suede shoes at home"
- "how to clean suede with baking soda"

Each one is a content opportunity.

2. **People Also Ask Box**

Located mid-SERP, this feature shows real questions people ask. Every one is a potential blog post, FAQ, or section in your content.

3. AnswerThePublic

This tool gives a visual map of questions and comparisons. It's great for brainstorming and spotting angles you might miss.

4. Free Tiers of Paid Tools

- Ahrefs Webmaster Tools (free for your site)
- Ubersuggest
- SEMRush's free queries

These tools give you:

- Keyword volume
- Difficulty scores
- Trends over time
- Competitor data

5. Your Own Brain

Seriously. Ask yourself:

- What would I Google if I needed this?
- What frustrations would I be trying to solve?
- What words would I use if I wasn't an expert?

Write them down. These are often your most valuable keywords—because they come from the customer's mindset.

A Framework for Organizing Your Keywords

Once you start gathering ideas, your list can get overwhelming fast. Don't let it spiral into chaos.

Use a simple spreadsheet or Notion table with the following columns: keywords, intent, volume, difficulty, URL idea.

Use filters to group by:

- Intent type
- Topic cluster
- Priority level

Mini Exercise: Build Your First Keyword List

1. Pick a topic related to your business.
   Example: "Home office furniture"
2. Use Google Search, People Also Ask, and one keyword tool
   Write down:
   - 5 short-tail keywords
   - 10 long-tail keywords

       ○   3 common questions
3. Add search intent to each

(Informational / Navigational / Transactional)

4. Mark which ones you want to create content for next

Checklist: What You Should Have After This Chapter

- 10–20 keywords with clear search intent
- Mix of short- and long-tail keywords
- At least 3 topics you can create content around
- Basic spreadsheet or Notion board to organize them
- An understanding of what your *audience* actually wants

Recap: SEO in 60 Seconds – Keyword Edition

- Start with intent, not volume
- Long-tail = higher chance of ranking
- Use Google, your tools, and your brain
- Study your competitors—but do it better
- Build a keyword list you can actually act on

Coming Up Next:
Now that you've got your keyword list, we're going to use it. In

Chapter 4, we'll look at how to craft content that ranks and converts—with Google's E-E-A-T principles baked in.

Chapter 4: Crafting High-Quality Content with E-E-A-T

Google doesn't just rank content. It ranks content it trusts.

If you've ever wondered why two pages with the same keywords can rank worlds apart, it often comes down to one thing: E-E-A-T.

That's Google's shorthand for Experience, Expertise, Authoritativeness, and Trustworthiness. It's not a ranking *algorithm*—but it influences how algorithms work. It's how Google judges if your content is written by someone who actually knows what they're talking about and whether users can trust what's on the page.

Most sites fail here. They write generic fluff, outsource blog posts to AI or content farms, and forget that users want to learn from *people*, not keyword bots. This chapter is about changing that.

What is E-E-A-T, Really?

Let's break it down:

Experience

Have you *actually done the thing* you're talking about?

- If you're reviewing products—have you used them?
- If you're writing about travel—have you been there?
- If you're giving advice—have you lived it?

Google wants first-hand knowledge. You don't need a PhD—just proof you've *been there, done that*.

Expertise

Do you have the knowledge to talk about this topic?

This matters more in fields like health, finance, or law ("YMYL" = *Your Money or Your Life* topics). But even in lifestyle niches, Google can smell shallow content.

Show your expertise by:

- Citing sources
- Using the right terminology
- Going deep, not wide

Authoritativeness

Are you recognized as a go-to source?
This comes from:

- Backlinks from trusted sites
- Mentions online

- Writing on respected platforms
- Guest appearances, interviews, awards

If your name (or brand) appears around the web in the right context, that builds authority.

Trustworthiness

Does your site *look and feel* legit?

That includes:

- HTTPS (secure)
- Clear contact info
- Transparent policies (privacy, returns, terms)
- No shady ads, pop-ups, or broken links

Even fake "best of" lists written by AI can rank temporarily—but they drop fast. Google is watching.

If your content could be copied and pasted to a competitor's site without anyone noticing—it's not good enough.

Writing for Humans First, Search Engines Second

Here's the mistake most people make: they start with keywords.
 Here's what *you* should do instead: start with the reader.

Ask yourself:

- What's the user really looking for?
- What's missing from the top-ranking results?
- Can I make this more actionable, faster to skim, or more personal?

Then—and only then—do you go back and optimize.

Google rewards content that actually *helps* people. And if your users love your page, they stay longer, click deeper, share more. That sends ranking signals *way stronger* than keyword density ever could.

Think "searcher satisfaction." If someone clicks your post, finds exactly what they needed, and leaves feeling smarter—you win.

Establishing Author Expertise (Even If You're Not Famous)

Not everyone's a published author or thought leader. That's fine.

You can still build credibility on your site with a few simple tricks:

- Add author bios to blog posts (mention your background, experience, or why you're qualified)
- Link to other articles you've written on the topic
- Share real-life examples or stories
- Don't hide behind "admin" or "team"—use your name and face

If you're in a niche where trust is key (health, finance, parenting), these details matter even more.

 If your blog posts are ghostwritten by random freelancers or AI with no byline, you're sending Google the message: "We don't really care who writes this."

Building Trust On-Page

Here's the part most marketers skip. Google doesn't just scan your text—it evaluates your entire page.

Trust signals to include:

- SSL (secure site)
- Real address and phone number
- Return/refund policies (if selling)
- Clear navigation and design
- No spelling or grammar errors
- No intrusive ads, popups, or clickbait headlines

Even having a "Meet the Team" page helps. Trust isn't one big checkbox—it's dozens of small signals that add up.

Content Format: Structure = Success

You can have the best info in the world, but if it's a giant wall of text? Nobody's reading it.

Structure helps both users and search engines understand your content.

Here's the basic formula:

- Clear H1 title

    → Includes main keyword

- Intro paragraph

    → Sets up what you're going to cover

- Subheadings (H2, H3)

    → Break up the content into chunks

- Bullet points and lists

    → For skimmability

- Images, videos, diagrams

    → Reinforce the message

- Call-to-action

    → Tell the reader what to do next (read more, buy now, sign up)

Every piece of content should solve a specific problem and give a clear next step.

Mini Exercise: Grade Your Own Content

Pick a blog post or page on your site and ask:

- Does this show first-hand experience or expertise?
- Would someone trust this content if they landed on it cold?
- Could this be improved with a story, source, quote, or visual?
- Is the structure easy to skim?
- Can I add an author bio, trust element, or resource?

Make small changes. Watch what happens to rankings in a few weeks.

Checklist: Your E-E-A-T Content Baseline

- Content shows first-hand experience
- Author name + short bio included
- No AI-generated junk or vague waffle
- Trust elements are visible (SSL, policies, real contact info)
- Clear structure: headings, paragraphs, bullet points
- Content satisfies the search intent fully
- Zero spelling/grammar mistakes
- No dark patterns or shady popups

Recap: Google Wants Content That's...

- Written by real people
- Trustworthy and helpful
- Easy to read and navigate
- Full of signals that show credibility

Coming Up Next:

In the next chapter, we'll look at the tech side of on-page SEO: meta tags, HTML basics, and how to speak Google's language. You'll learn how to optimize your titles, descriptions, headers, and images *without sounding like a robot*.

Chapter 5: Meta Tags and HTML Basics

Because even the best content gets ignored if Google can't read it right.

So, you've got a killer piece of content. It's helpful, it's clear, it's packed with E-E-A-T. But here's the thing: if your title tag sucks, your meta description is missing, or your HTML structure looks like spaghetti code... Google's going to skip it—or rank it poorly.

Imagine your content as a shop on a busy street. The meta title is your storefront sign. The meta description is the pitch in the window. They don't just help Google understand your page—they help users decide whether or not to *click*.

In many cases, these 160 characters are the only chance you get to convince someone to visit your site. And yet, countless websites either leave them blank, duplicate them across pages, or write something so generic it might as well say "Page Title Here."

If you want to increase visibility and engagement, start with your meta tags.

This chapter is about making sure both Google and your audience know exactly what your page is about at a glance.

Let's break down the essentials.

What Is a Meta Title?

A meta title (a.k.a. title tag) is the headline that shows up as the blue clickable link in search engine results. It's also used as the tab name in browsers and the default title when sharing on social media.

Search engines use this tag as a strong ranking signal. But more importantly, users use it as their first filtering decision.

Best Practices for Meta Titles:

- Include the primary keyword (early if possible)
- Be descriptive, not vague
- Add context (brand, location, product spec, etc.)
- Keep it under 60 characters to avoid truncation
- Make it unique for every page

Weak Meta Title Examples:

- *Home*
- *Product Page | My Store*
- *Welcome to Our Blog*

These tell neither Google nor the user what the page is about.

Strong Meta Title Examples:

- *Affordable Ergonomic Office Chairs | Free UK Delivery*
- *How to Clean Suede Shoes Without Ruining Them – Expert Guide*
- *B2B SEO Strategy for 2025 | Complete Framework + Templates*

Each of these:

- Speaks directly to the search query
- Conveys value or relevance
- Signals intent clearly (e.g., "guide," "expert," "affordable")

Pro tip: Don't just match keywords—match searcher expectations.

 If your title tag sounds like a filing cabinet label, you're doing it wrong. Give people a reason to click—not just a label to read.

What Is a Meta Description?

The meta description appears beneath your title in search results. While Google doesn't always use your written meta description (sometimes it rewrites one based on page content), a well-crafted description *usually sticks* and can significantly boost your click-through rate (CTR).

It's not a ranking factor directly, but it drives clicks, which affects user engagement signals—*and that can affect rankings over time.*

Best Practices for Meta Descriptions:

- Stay between 140–160 characters
- Include main and secondary keywords (naturally)
- Use active, compelling language
- Highlight a benefit, feature, or differentiator
- Include a clear CTA (Shop, Learn, Read, Try)

Real Meta Description Comparisons

Bad Meta Description:

"Check out our product page for more details. Great quality and prices."

- Too vague
- Lacks a keyword
- Sounds like filler text

Better Meta Description:

"Explore our handpicked selection of ergonomic office chairs designed for posture support and productivity. Free delivery across the UK."

- Hits the keyword ("ergonomic office chairs")
- Describes the benefit (posture support, productivity)
- Offers a compelling extra (free delivery)

Think of the meta description as your elevator pitch. If someone only sees one sentence about your business—this is it.

Ecommerce Example:

Title:

Luxury Scented Candles | Hand-Poured in the UK – Amber & Cedar

Description:
"Shop our artisan collection of eco-friendly, hand-poured candles. Clean burn. Long-lasting scent. Made in Yorkshire with sustainable soy wax."

Why it works:

- Includes keywords like *hand-poured candles*
- Focuses on product qualities: eco-friendly, clean burn, scent longevity
- Builds trust with specifics (Made in Yorkshire)

Blog Example:

Title:

How to Build Topical Authority in 2025 – SEO Strategy Guide

Description:

"Learn how to structure your site and content to dominate a niche using topical authority. Real examples, free checklist included."

Why it works:

- Focused on *how-to* intent
- Hints at depth (structure, strategy, checklist)
- Incentivizes the click with a free resource

Writing Meta Tags for Different Page Types

Homepage:

Should summarize what your brand offers and who it's for.

- *Bespoke Furniture for Modern Homes | Handmade in the UK*
- *Digital Marketing for Startups | SEO, PPC & Content Services*

Product Pages:

Highlight key features and benefits.

- *Organic Cotton T-Shirts | Soft, Durable & Eco-Friendly*
- *4K Ultra HD Smart TV | Dolby Vision, 55-Inch, WiFi Built-In*

Service Pages:

Focus on outcomes, location, and specialization.

- *Freelance SEO Consultant | UK-Based Expert with 10+ Years' Experience*
- *Local Plumber in Leeds | Fast Response | No Callout Fees*

Blog Posts:

Use clear, actionable titles. Let readers know what they'll gain.

- *SEO Checklist for New Websites – Setup & Optimization Guide*
- *10 Myths About Keyword Density (And What to Do Instead)*

How to Test & Improve Meta Tags Over Time

Meta titles and descriptions are not set-it-and-forget-it. They can and should be tested, tracked, and refined for better performance.

Tools to Help:

- Google Search Console → Check impressions vs. clicks. Pages with low CTRs might need stronger titles/descriptions.
- Yoast / RankMath (WordPress) → Helps format and preview meta tags in CMS.
- Ahrefs or SEMrush → Track SERP positions and competitor meta formats.

Pro Tip: Use Google's search preview tool or plugins to see how your meta tags will appear in real search results. Also, try Googling this to check existing meta tags:

site:yourwebsite.com

Beyond Meta Tags: Why HTML Structure Still Matters

Even in 2025, Google's crawlers rely on good old-fashioned HTML to understand your pages. While JavaScript-heavy sites and visual builders are more common now, clear HTML tags remain the backbone of solid SEO.

Why? Because Google scans your code *before* it sees your design. It's trying to figure out:

- What the page is about
- Which parts are important
- How the information is organized

If your HTML is messy or misused, you create confusion. Confusion leads to poor rankings.

Let's fix that.

Header Tags: Give Your Content a Clear Outline

Header tags (H1, H2, H3, etc.) are more than just formatting tools. They're signposts—they tell Google (and users) how your content is structured.

Think of them like the table of contents in a book.

How They Work:

- **H1** = Main page topic (only one per page)
- **H2s** = Major sections
- **H3s** = Sub-sections within each H2
- And so on...

Good structure example:

H1: The Complete Guide to Home Office Design

- H2: Choosing the Right Desk

  - H3: Corner Desks vs. Standing Desks

  - H3: Material Considerations

- H2: Lighting Your Space

  - H3: Natural vs. Artificial Light

  - H3: LED Desk Lamps for Focus

Bad structure example: Using multiple H1s, skipping levels (e.g., H2 to H4), or using bold text instead of actual header tags.

Tips for Writing SEO-Friendly Headers

- Make them scannable: People should be able to skim and still understand your page.
- Include keywords naturally, especially in H1s and H2s.
- Keep them short, clear, and to the point.
- Avoid stuffing them with exact-match phrases—it's not 2010 anymore.

Don't force keywords. Write for clarity, then optimize subtly.

Image Alt Text: Accessibility Meets SEO

Google still can't "see" images—it reads the surrounding code, especially the alt attribute.

Alt text serves two critical roles:

1. Accessibility: Screen readers use it to describe images to visually impaired users.
2. SEO: It helps Google understand what the image shows, which can improve relevance and rankings (especially in Google Images).

How to Write Great Alt Text:

- Be descriptive: Say what's actually in the image.
- Be accurate: Don't stuff it with unrelated keywords.
- Be concise: One sentence max.

Bad Alt Text:

`image123.jpg` or `"product photo"`

Good Alt Text:

`"Modern oak dining table with metal legs in minimalist room"`

If the image is decorative or purely visual (e.g., background pattern), it's okay to leave the alt empty (`alt=""`) to avoid redundancy for screen readers.

Common HTML Mistakes (and Easy Fixes)

1. **Multiple H1s per page**
   - Solution: Keep it to **one H1**, then use H2s, H3s, etc. appropriately.

2. **No alt text on images**
   - Add descriptive alt tags on *all important visuals*, especially products, diagrams, and blog visuals.

3. **Missing or generic title tags**
   - Every page needs a unique, keyword-relevant title. Avoid "Home" or "Welcome."

4. **Meta description left blank or duplicated across pages**
   - Write a custom, relevant meta description for each major page. Don't copy/paste.

5. **Using bold or font-size increases instead of header tags**
   - Visual formatting ≠ HTML structure. Use `<h2>`, not just `<strong>`.

6. **Unnecessary HTML bloat from page builders**

○ If using WordPress, Shopify, or Webflow, check your source code. Remove unused CSS, scripts, or nested divs when possible.

HTML Tools for Non-Coders

You don't need to write raw code to get clean HTML. These tools help you stay on top of your page structure:

- Screaming Frog SEO Spider → View header structure across your site
- SEO Minion (Chrome Extension) → See title, meta description, headers, and alt text at a glance
- Web Developer Tools (Browser) → View source or inspect elements easily

And for accessibility testing:

- axe Accessibility Tool or WAVE Evaluation Tool – highlights missing alt text and ARIA roles

Even one missing alt or misused header can weaken your SEO if repeated site-wide.

Recap: HTML + Meta = SEO Fundamentals Done Right

If content is your message, meta tags and HTML structure are how it's delivered. When everything aligns—your titles, your headers, your image descriptions—you're giving both Google and your visitors a *smooth, trustworthy experience.*

Canonical Tags: Your Shield Against Duplicate Content

Search engines don't like guessing games. When they find multiple versions of the same content across different URLs, they get confused—which one should they rank? Which one is the "original"? If you don't guide them, they might:

- Split your ranking power between those versions
- Choose the wrong one to index
- Or worse, drop them all from results

That's where the canonical tag comes in.

Adding `rel="canonical"` to your page tells Google: *"Hey, this is the main version. Please ignore the duplicates."*

When You Need a Canonical Tag

Use canonical tags when:

- You have pagination (e.g., `/blog?page=2`, `/blog?page=3`)
- Your products have variants that create multiple URLs (e.g., `/blue-shirt` and `/blue-shirt?size=medium`)
- The same content exists in multiple categories (e.g., `/mens/jackets` and `/winter/jackets`)
- You use URL parameters for sorting, tracking, or filtering (e.g., `/laptops?sort=price`)

Even if the content looks similar to humans, to Google it's a different URL—and that can cause trouble.

Good News: Your CMS Might Be Handling It Already

Popular platforms like Shopify, Webflow, and WordPress often insert canonical tags automatically. But don't assume—it's worth checking manually or using a tool like:

- Ahrefs Site Audit
- Screaming Frog
- Yoast SEO plugin (WordPress)
- Google Search Console → URL Inspection Tool

What a Canonical Tag Looks Like in Code

It lives in the `<head>` of your HTML:

```
<link rel="canonical"
href="https://www.example.com/main-page" />
```

This tells Google: "No matter how someone lands here, treat *this* URL as the primary version."

If you're intentionally duplicating content (say for A/B testing or geo-targeting), using canonical tags can help you avoid SEO penalties while still providing tailored experiences.

Mini Exercise: Clean Up One Page's Metadata

Pick one of your pages or blog posts and do a mini audit:

1. Is there a clear, unique title tag?
2. Does the meta description tell people why to click?
3. Is there only one H1, with logical H2/H3?
4. Do your images have alt text?
5. If you have similar pages—do they use canonical tags?

Make improvements, then use tools to double check your structure.

Checklist: Your On-Page HTML Must-Haves

- Unique, keyword-optimized title tag under 60 characters
- Compelling meta description under 160 characters
- One H1 tag per page
- Logical header hierarchy (H2, H3, etc.)
- Alt text on all images
- Canonical tags used (if needed)
- Clean, readable HTML without unnecessary div spam

Recap: Speak Google's Language Without Sounding Robotic

- Title tags = first impression
- Meta descriptions = reason to click
- Header tags = structure and clarity
- Alt text = image context + accessibility
- Canonical tags = prevent content confusion

If E-E-A-T is your *voice*, HTML is your *grammar*. Use both well, and Google will listen.

Coming Up Next:

Now that we've structured your content, let's teach your site how to talk directly to Google's brain: Chapter 6 is all about Schema Markup—what it is, how it works, and why it gives you a serious edge.

Chapter 6: Schema Markup – Speaking Google's Language

Want better rankings, higher click-throughs, and rich results? Talk to Google in its own language.

Imagine walking into a room full of people and shouting, "I'm interesting, I swear!" Now imagine walking into the same room, handing out a neatly organized flyer that explains *exactly* who you are, what you do, what people say about you, and what problems you solve.

That flyer is schema.

Schema markup is a type of structured data—code that helps search engines understand your content better. It doesn't replace good content or SEO basics—but it enhances them. It's the difference between being seen and being understood.

What Is Schema, Exactly?

Schema is code (usually in JSON-LD format) that adds context to your content.

To humans, your page might clearly be about a recipe or a product. But to Google, without structure, it's just a blob of text.

Schema makes things crystal clear. It helps Google understand:

- What your content *is*
- Who it's for
- What entities (people, places, things) are involved

This clarity helps you qualify for rich results like:

- Review stars
- FAQs
- Product prices
- Event dates
- Author info
- Videos and recipe cards

 If you're not using schema, you're leaving easy traffic and higher click-through rates on the table. This isn't optional anymore—it's expected.

Types of Schema You Should Actually Care About

There are hundreds of schema types, but you don't need all of them. Just the ones that align with your content and goals.

Here's what matters most:

Organization / Local Business

Tells Google who you are.

- Name, logo, social profiles, address
- For local SEO, use LocalBusiness with opening hours, service areas, etc.

Article / BlogPosting

Adds context to blog content.

- Author, datePublished, headline, image, word count
- Also supports breadcrumb and AMP metadata

Product

Essential for eCommerce.

- Name, price, brand, availability, rating, SKU
- Enables rich product snippets in SERPs

Review / AggregateRating

If you display reviews, you can show stars in SERPs.
Make sure they're real—and displayed on the page too
(Google checks).

FAQPage

You've seen those expandable FAQs in search?
That's this. Only use it for *actual* FAQs—not just as a hack.

BreadcrumbList

Improves site structure in search results—especially helpful
on large sites.

Event, Course, JobPosting, Recipe, Video

Use if they apply to your content directly. They trigger rich
displays like event calendars, video previews, or recipe cards.

Don't force schema where it doesn't
belong. Google has started cracking down
on spammy or misused markup. Only use it
if it reflects real content on the page.

How to Add Schema (Without Losing Your Mind)

There are three ways to implement schema:

1. **JSON-LD** (Recommended)

A script added to the or of your page.
 Clean, easy to manage, and officially recommended by Google.

Example:

2. **Microdata / RDFa**

Old-school inline markup inside your HTML elements. Not recommended unless your CMS requires it.

3. **Plugins and Tools**

For WordPress: RankMath, Yoast (basic schema)
For Shopify: Use apps or insert custom code via Liquid
Webflow: Add JSON-LD in Embed elements or via settings
Custom-built sites: You're free to go wild

Tools for Writing and Testing Schema

- Google's Rich Results Test – Checks if your schema is valid and eligible for enhancements
- Schema Markup Validator – Replaces the old Structured Data Testing Tool
- Merkle's Schema Generator – Easy point-and-click builder
- JSONLint – Helps you fix errors in formatting

 If your schema contains fake ratings, invisible content, or markup that doesn't match the page—Google will penalize you.

Every Page That Matters Needs Schema

Let me make this painfully clear: if you want a page to rank, it needs schema.

Homepage? Needs Organization or LocalBusiness schema.
Product pages? Absolutely need more than just Product.
Blog posts? Need Article, Breadcrumb, and maybe FAQ.
Service pages? You guessed it—LocalBusiness, Service, and
WebPage.

If Google doesn't fully understand what your page is, it won't
rank it well.

Product Pages Need More Than Just Product Schema

This is a common mistake: people think adding Product and
Offer is enough. But real-world SEO needs more depth.

Every serious product page should include:

- Product and Offer (name, price, availability, SKU, etc.)
- Review and AggregateRating (if you collect reviews)
- FAQPage (if you have a Q&A or common customer questions)
- Organization or LocalBusiness schema (adds context about *who* is selling the product)

Schema plugins? Burn them. They create the illusion that "it's all taken care of," when really, they're doing the bare minimum—and often doing it wrong. If you want schema done right, code it yourself (or use CMS variables if available).

Use Dynamic Variables (Like Shopify's Liquid)

Here's the good news: you don't need to manually write schema for every product.
If you're using Shopify, Webflow, or another CMS that supports variables—you can add schema once to your product template, and it will automatically populate for every item.

For example, in Shopify's Liquid language, you'd pull in:

- {{ product.title }}
- {{ product.price }}
- {{ product.vendor }}
- {{ product.variants.first.sku }}
  ...and so on.

One schema block, infinite products.

If your CMS allows it—utilize it. If not, it might be time to upgrade.

The Homepage: Your SEO Foundation

Your homepage is where trust begins. It sets the tone for both users and Google. That's why it deserves a full-stack, hand-coded schema setup—not just a line that says "We're an organization, trust us."

Here's what your homepage should include:

Recommended Schema Types for Homepages:

- Organization or LocalBusiness (whichever is more accurate)
- WebSite – lets you define a site-wide search action
- WebPage – gives Google info about the specific page
- ContactPoint – helps link phone/email to departments
- SocialProfile – use sameAs to link Instagram, Facebook, etc.
- PostalAddress – tied to LocalBusiness
- Business hours, logo, founder/owner (if relevant)

If you care about rankings and trust, your homepage schema should feel like a Google CV—clean, structured, and detailed.

Full JSON-LD Example for Homepage

Here's an ultra-complete homepage schema for a fictional business called *Oak & Iron*—a furniture company with both online and physical presence.

```
<script type="application/ld+json">

{

  "@context": "https://schema.org",

  "@graph": [

    /* ORGANIZATION / LOCAL BUSINESS */

    {

      "@type": "LocalBusiness",

      "@id": "https://oakandiron.com/#business",

      "name": "Oak & Iron",

      "image": "https://oakandiron.com/logo.png",
```

```
"url": "https://oakandiron.com",

"description": "Oak & Iron is a UK-based
retailer of handcrafted wooden furniture, blending
rustic charm with modern design.",

"telephone": "+44-113-123-4567",

"email": "support@oakandiron.com",

"priceRange": "££",

"address": {

  "@type": "PostalAddress",

  "streetAddress": "15 Market Street",

  "addressLocality": "Leeds",

  "postalCode": "LS1 5PL",

  "addressCountry": "GB"

},

"geo": {

  "@type": "GeoCoordinates",

  "latitude": "53.797418",

  "longitude": "-1.543794"

},

"openingHours": [
```

```
      "Mo-Fr 10:00-18:00",

      "Sa 10:00-17:00",

      "Su Closed"

    ],

    "sameAs": [

      "https://www.instagram.com/oakandiron",

      "https://www.facebook.com/oakandiron",

      "https://www.pinterest.com/oakandiron"

    ]

  },

  /* WEBSITE SCHEMA */

  {

    "@type": "WebSite",

    "@id": "https://oakandiron.com/#website",

    "url": "https://oakandiron.com",

    "name": "Oak & Iron",

    "publisher": {

      "@id": "https://oakandiron.com/#business"

    },
```

```
    "potentialAction": {

      "@type": "SearchAction",

      "target":
"https://oakandiron.com/search?q={search_term_strin
g}",

      "query-input": "required
name=search_term_string"

    }

  },

  /* HOMEPAGE SCHEMA */

  {

    "@type": "WebPage",

    "@id": "https://oakandiron.com/#webpage",

    "url": "https://oakandiron.com",

    "name": "Oak & Iron | Handcrafted Wooden
Furniture",

    "description": "Discover handcrafted oak
furniture designed for modern living. Shop dining
tables, coffee tables, and bedroom essentials with
UK-wide delivery.",

    "inLanguage": "en-GB",

    "isPartOf": {
```

```
      "@id": "https://oakandiron.com/#website"
    },
    "about": {
      "@id": "https://oakandiron.com/#business"
    },
    "primaryImageOfPage": {
      "@type": "ImageObject",
      "url":
"https://oakandiron.com/images/showroom.jpg"
    },
    "datePublished": "2023-01-01",
    "dateModified": "2025-03-26"
  }
  ]
}
</script>
```

Where to Place This Schema

- If your site has a layout or theme file (like theme.liquid in Shopify or a block in Webflow/Next.js), place the Organization/LocalBusiness schema in there or in the header file so it loads site-wide.
- Do not duplicate this schema block inside product, blog, or service page schema—just reference it via @id if needed.

On Product Pages: Just Reference, Don't Duplicate

Once you've added your Organization or LocalBusiness schema globally (to layout or template), don't repeat it inside product page schema.

Instead, in your Product > offers > seller, reference the ID like this:

```
"seller": {

"@id": "https://oakandiron.com/#business"

}
```

This keeps your schema cleaner, avoids duplication penalties, and helps Google see the connection between all your pages and your brand.

Mini Exercise: Add or Audit Schema on One Page

Choose one of your core pages (homepage, product page, or blog post) and:

1. Open Google's Rich Results Test
2. Paste in your URL
3. See what schema is detected
4. Use a generator to add missing types (e.g. Product, Article, LocalBusiness)
5. Add it to your site via CMS, plugin, or code
6. Re-test it to confirm

Checklist: Schema Done Right

- Schema reflects actual content on the page
- JSON-LD format used (cleanest option)
- At least one core schema type applied (e.g. Product, Article, LocalBusiness)
- Rich Results Test passed with no warnings
- Ratings or reviews are real and visible

- Not misused to manipulate SERPs

Recap: Schema Isn't Optional—It's a Competitive Edge

- It helps search engines understand your content
- It enables rich results that increase click-through rates
- It's easy to implement with the right tools
- It's your way of saying, "Hey Google—this is what I actually offer."

Coming Up Next:
Now that you've told Google what each page is about, let's teach it how to connect them. Chapter 7 is all about Internal Linking—a strategy that's boring to most, but powerful as hell when done right.

Chapter 7: Internal Linking – Connecting Your Site for Users and Google

Think of your site like a city. Internal links are the roads that connect everything. No roads = no traffic.

Internal linking is one of the most powerful, underutilized SEO tactics out there. People obsess over backlinks but ignore their own site's structure. Bad move.

When you link strategically between your own pages, you help Google:

- Discover new content faster
- Understand which pages are important
- Pass ranking power (a.k.a. link equity)
- Create topic clusters that signal authority

And you help users:

- Stay on your site longer
- Navigate more easily
- Find the info they didn't know they needed

Win-win.

What Is an Internal Link? (And Why Google Cares)

An internal link is simply a link from one page on your site to another page on your site.

That could be:

- A navigation link
- A link in your footer
- A contextual link in your content ("Learn more about wooden bed frames")
- A button, card, or CTA

Google crawls your site by following these links—just like a user would. The more connected your pages are, the easier it is for Google to index and rank them.

 Pages with no internal links pointing to them are called orphan pages. If Google can't find them, they might as well not exist.

Anchor Text Matters (More Than You Think)

Anchor text is the clickable part of the link. It tells Google *and the user* what they'll get if they click.

Best practices:

- Be descriptive, not vague

  → "See our bedroom storage options" beats "Click here"

- Include keywords naturally

  → But don't overdo it with exact-match spam

- Keep it short and clear

  → No one wants to read a whole sentence as a link

If every internal link uses the same keyword-rich anchor (e.g. "cheap sofas UK"), Google will see it as manipulation. Mix it up.

Create a Logical Internal Structure

Internal links shouldn't be random—they should be purposeful and hierarchical.

Start with:

- Homepage → links to core categories or key pages
- Category pages → link to individual product or article pages
- Blog posts → link to each other and relevant product pages
- Pillar pages → link out to "spoke" or supporting content

You're building what's called a topic cluster: one main page (pillar) that links to and from smaller, related pages.

Example:

Pillar Page: "Ultimate Guide to Home Office Furniture"

→ Links out to:

- "Best Ergonomic Chairs Under £200"
- "How to Set Up Your Desk for Posture"
- "Home Office Layout Ideas for Small Spaces"

Each of those should also link back to the pillar. Now Google sees a strong topic signal.

Where to Add Internal Links (and How Many)

Add links:

- In the body of blog posts and pages
- At the end of articles (related reads)
- Inside product descriptions (when relevant)
- In FAQs or support docs
- Even in breadcrumbs

There's no "perfect number," but a good rule of thumb:
Every page should link to 2–5 other pages.
And every important page should be linked to from multiple places.

You should be intentional. Don't just link because you can—link because it helps the user or builds the authority of another page.

How to Find Internal Linking Opportunities

If your site's already live, here's how to optimize:

1. Make a list of your most valuable pages (money pages, lead magnets, high-converting content)
2. Go through your existing blog posts or content
3. Find places where you naturally mention topics that relate to those money pages
4. Add a contextual link

Tools that help:

- Ahrefs > Site Audit > Link Opportunities
- Screaming Frog – shows internal link counts per page
- Google Search Console > Links – helps identify what pages get the most internal links (and which get none)

Mini Exercise: Build Your First Topic Cluster

Pick one of your service or product categories and map it out:

1. Main (pillar) page

   e.g. "Dining Room Furniture"

2. Create a list of supporting pages/posts
   - "Best Extendable Dining Tables for Small Homes"
   - "Dining Chair Trends 2025"
   - "Round vs Rectangle Tables: Which Fits Better?"

3. Link from the pillar to each post

4. Link from each post back to the pillar

5. Add natural internal links between related posts

Boom. You've just created your first internal SEO spiderweb.

Checklist: Internal Linking That Works

- Every important page is linked to from 2+ places
- Anchor text is varied and descriptive
- Topic clusters exist around core products/services
- No orphan pages
- Internal links help users find more, not get lost

- Internal link structure flows logically from top to bottom

Recap: Small Links, Big Impact

- Internal links help both Google and users navigate
- Good anchor text and structure = higher rankings
- Build topic clusters to dominate a niche
- Every link should have a purpose, not just a keyword

Coming Up Next:
We're switching gears in the next part of the book: Technical SEO. Starting with site speed—because if your pages take forever to load, all the keywords and content in the world won't save you.

Chapter 8: Website Speed and Performance

You can't rank if users bounce before your page even loads.

You've probably done it yourself—clicked on a result, waited a few seconds, and then hit back before the page even finished loading. That right there is why speed matters. A slow site doesn't just frustrate users—it bleeds traffic, conversions, and SEO value.

Google has explicitly said that site speed is a ranking factor—especially on mobile. And with the rise of Core Web Vitals, it's now baked into the algorithm.

This chapter is about identifying speed issues and fixing them *without needing to be a developer.*

Why Site Speed Is SEO Rocket Fuel

When someone lands on your site, you've got about 2–3 seconds to impress them—or they'll bounce.

And it's not just about user frustration. Google has publicly stated that site speed is a ranking factor. A slow website leads to:

- Lower rankings
- Higher bounce rates
- Poor conversion rates
- Lower engagement (especially on mobile)

In other words, a sluggish website makes you invisible *and* untrustworthy.

What Affects Your Site's Speed?

You don't need to be a developer to speed things up. But you do need to know what matters most.

Key factors that influence page load speed:

- Image size and format
- Too many scripts and plugins
- Web hosting quality
- No caching setup
- Render-blocking CSS/JavaScript
- Uncompressed code
- Poor mobile responsiveness

Tools to Measure Site Speed

Use these tools to get a real performance score (not just your gut feeling):

- **Google PageSpeed Insights**
  → Gives mobile/desktop speed scores and

  diagnostics

- **GTmetrix**
  → Visual waterfall breakdown of load steps

- **WebPageTest.org**
  → Advanced timings and filmstrip view

- **Lighthouse (Chrome DevTools)**
  → Integrated audit tool in Chrome browser

Lazy vs. Eager Loading: Why It Matters

This is where many non-technical site owners get tripped up—especially on image-heavy pages.

Eager Loading

By default, most websites eager load every image, video, and element as soon as the page starts loading—even if it's way below the fold (not visible yet).

This results in:

- Longer total load times
- Bigger upfront data transfer
- Unnecessary strain on bandwidth

Lazy Loading

With lazy loading, only the content in view loads first. Everything else waits until the user scrolls to it.

This results in:

- Faster perceived load
- Less bandwidth use
- Better Core Web Vitals scores

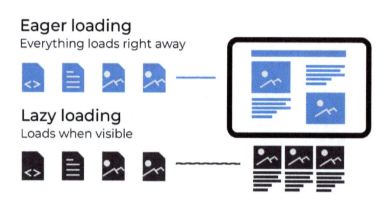

Eager loading
Everything loads right away

Lazy loading
Loads when visible

Lazy loading delays images below the fold, speeding up the visible part of your site.

How to Enable Lazy Loading

If you're using WordPress or Shopify, you don't need to touch code:

- **WordPress:**
    - Use plugins like WP Rocket, Smush, or Native Lazy Load
    - WordPress 5.5+ supports lazy loading natively for images

- **Shopify / Webflow:**
  - Use built-in settings or third-party optimizers
  - Set image tags with `loading="lazy"` manually or via theme

```
<img src="image.jpg" loading="lazy" alt="Alt
description" />
```

What Else Should You Optimize?

Here's a checklist you can follow without breaking your site:

- **Compress images**
  Use tools like TinyPNG, Squoosh, or plugins that auto-optimize on upload.
- **Use modern image formats**
  Serve images as WebP or AVIF where possible—smaller files, same quality.
- **Minify CSS, JS, and HTML**
  Shrink your code and remove unnecessary whitespace/comments.
- **Enable caching**
  Browser caching helps repeat visitors load your site faster.

- **Use a CDN**

  A Content Delivery Network like Cloudflare stores copies of your site on servers worldwide for faster delivery.

- **Limit third-party scripts**

  Remove unnecessary embeds, widgets, trackers, and social share buttons.

- **Avoid bloated page builders**

  They're handy, but too many plugins or bloated themes can make your site crawl.

- **Host with performance in mind**

  Shared hosting may be cheap—but it's often painfully slow. Invest in quality.

Mobile Speed Matters Most

Most searches happen on mobile now—and Google indexes *mobile-first*. If your site is fast on desktop but a nightmare on phones, your rankings and UX will suffer.

 Run your site through PageSpeed Insights and focus first on the mobile score. That's what Google sees first.

When to Stop Optimizing

Don't get stuck chasing a perfect 100 score. Focus on:

- Loading under 3 seconds
- Cumulative Layout Shift (CLS) and Largest Contentful Paint (LCP) scores
- Real-world experience, not just lab scores

Sometimes improving by 5% means rewriting half your site—for no noticeable gain. Prioritize high-impact wins first.

```
Slow websites are like leaky funnels.
You pour in traffic—ads, SEO, referrals—
and it just drips away. Fix your speed,
plug the hole.
```

How to Measure Site Speed (Without Guessing)

Use these tools to get real performance data:

1. Google PageSpeed Insights

- Gives you both mobile and desktop scores
- Highlights Core Web Vitals: LCP (load speed), FID (interactivity), CLS (layout shifts)
- Offers actionable suggestions

2. GTmetrix

- Loads your site from different global locations
- Shows waterfall chart of loading behavior
- Great for visual learners

3. WebPageTest.org

- Offers more granular data, like Time to First Byte (TTFB)
- Useful for diagnosing server-level issues

4. Chrome DevTools > Performance Tab

- See what's happening under the hood in real time
- Spot render-blocking scripts and layout shifts

Run these tests on your most important pages (homepage, product pages, blog posts). Don't just test your homepage and assume the rest is fine.

Common Speed Killers (and How to Fix Them)

Let's hit the big culprits:

1. Uncompressed or Oversized Images

- Use WebP or AVIF formats
- Compress with TinyPNG, Squoosh, or native CMS compression
- Resize to the exact size needed (don't load a 3000px image in a 300px box)

2. Unused JavaScript and CSS

- Remove code bloat from themes and plugins
- Only load scripts when needed (e.g. don't load your Instagram feed JS on every page)

- Use async/defer tags to load JS after the page content

3. Poor Hosting

- Shared hosting = slower speeds
- Choose a provider with servers close to your audience
- Consider a CDN (like Cloudflare) to cache and serve content faster globally

4. Render-Blocking Resources

- Inline critical CSS
- Move JavaScript to the bottom of the page (or load it asynchronously)
- Lazy-load images and iframes

5. Too Many Web Fonts

- Limit font weights and styles
- Use system fonts where possible
- Preload key fonts in your

If your homepage loads 60+ scripts and 5
different font families—your speed is
dying under the weight of your design.

Understanding Core Web Vitals

These are the three metrics Google uses to measure "page
experience":

- Largest Contentful Paint (LCP): measures load
  speed. Aim for less than 2.5 seconds.
- First Input Delay (FID): time before interaction is
  possible. Aim for less than 100ms.
- Cumulative Layout Shift (CLS): visual stability. Aim for
  less than 0.1

You can check these using PageSpeed Insights or in Google
Search Console under the "Core Web Vitals" report.

Speed Killers & Fixes Cheat Sheet

- **Images**
  - Killers: Oversized, uncompressed images; outdated formats (e.g., JPEG/PNG only).
  - Fixes: Compress images using tools like TinyPNG or Squoosh; convert to modern formats (WebP, AVIF); resize images to match display dimensions.

- **JavaScript & CSS**
  - Killers: Unused or render-blocking scripts and styles; excessive code bloat from plugins and themes.
  - Fixes: Remove or defer unused code; load scripts asynchronously (use async/defer tags); inline critical CSS.

- **Hosting & CDN**
  - Killers: Slow or unreliable hosting; distant server locations.
  - Fixes: Upgrade to high-performance hosting; use a CDN (e.g., Cloudflare) to serve content closer to users.

- **Web Fonts**

- Killers: Loading too many font families and weights; unoptimized font delivery.
- Fixes: Limit font usage to essential weights/styles; use system fonts when possible; preload key fonts in your .

- **Lazy Loading**
  - Killers: Loading all images and iframes on page load, causing delays.
  - Fixes: Implement lazy loading for images, videos, and iframes so they load only when in the viewport.

- **Render-Blocking Resources**
  - Killers: Critical resources that block page rendering (e.g., CSS and JS loaded in the without deferment).
  - Fixes: Inline critical CSS; defer non-essential scripts to load after the main content.

- **Core Web Vitals Monitoring**
  - Action: Regularly test pages using Google PageSpeed Insights or GTmetrix to check LCP, FID, and CLS.
  - Goal: Aim for LCP under 2.5 seconds, FID under 100ms, and CLS under 0.1.

Use this cheat sheet as a quick reference to diagnose and fix common speed issues. Regular testing and incremental improvements can lead to significant performance gains, better user experience, and improved SEO.

Mini Exercise: Speed Audit Your Site

1. Run your homepage, best blog post, and top product page through PageSpeed Insights
2. Write down:
   - Mobile vs desktop scores
   - LCP, FID, CLS
   - Top 3 issues flagged
3. Use a tool like GTmetrix or WebPageTest to cross-check results
4. Fix 1–2 things immediately: compress images, lazy-load videos, remove unnecessary apps/plugins

Even small tweaks can make a huge difference.

Checklist: Your Speed Optimization Baseline

- Images compressed and in modern formats (WebP/AVIF)
- Scripts and CSS optimized (no render-blocking)
- Fonts limited and properly loaded

- Lazy loading enabled for media
- CDN in place (Cloudflare or similar)
- Hosting is fast, reliable, and scalable
- Core Web Vitals are in the "green"
- Page loads fully in under 3 seconds (goal: 1.5s if possible)

Recap: Speed = SEO + UX + Conversions

- Site speed affects rankings, user experience, and sales
- You don't need to be a developer to fix most issues
- Use tools, test regularly, and improve page-by-page
- Don't let design or bloated code destroy your performance

Coming Up Next:
Now that your site is loading like a dream, let's make sure it works *everywhere*. Chapter 9 is all about Mobile Optimization—what it really means to be mobile-friendly (spoiler: it's not just responsive design).

Chapter 9: Mobile Optimization – Winning the Mobile-First Game

If your site's not mobile-first, it's not first at all.

We're way past the point where mobile design is optional. In fact, since 2020, Google has used mobile-first indexing by default—which means it's the mobile version of your site that gets crawled, indexed, and ranked. Not desktop.

So if your mobile experience is clunky, slow, broken, or missing content—you're not just annoying users… you're sabotaging your SEO.

This chapter is about building for thumbs, not mice, and making sure Google sees the best version of your site.

What Mobile-First Indexing Really Means

Google used to look at the desktop version of your site for ranking. Now, it looks at the mobile version first.

That means:

- If your mobile site is stripped down, missing schema, or content is hidden—it won't rank well.

- If your mobile experience is buggy or slow, Google notices.
- Mobile gets indexed first, ranked first, and sets the tone for everything.

Your site might look amazing on desktop...
...but if mobile is an afterthought, your SEO is toast.

 Mobile users aren't patient. If your site takes too long, has tiny buttons, or forces them to zoom—congrats, you just lost a sale and your ranking.

What "Mobile-Friendly" Really Means (It's Not Just Responsive)

Responsive design is the starting point, not the goal.

Being truly mobile-friendly means:

- Your site is fast on mobile (2–3s max)
- Navigation is thumb-friendly (buttons are tap-sized, menus are clear)
- Fonts are readable without pinching or zooming

- Tap targets are spaced properly
- No elements overlap or shift around
- Forms are easy to use, even with autocorrect off
- Content isn't hidden behind weird expandable sections unless necessary

Tools to test:

- Mobile-Friendly Test
- PageSpeed Insights (Mobile Tab)
- Chrome DevTools > Toggle Device Toolbar

Common Mobile SEO Mistakes

Let's list the big offenders:

✘ Desktop content hidden on mobile

→ If Google can't see it on mobile, it won't rank it.

✘ Slow load times

→ Especially with mobile networks. Optimize images, lazy-load, use CDN.

✗ Tiny text / tap targets

→ Google will literally flag this in Search Console. Fix font sizes and spacing.

✗ Full-screen pop-ups

→ Mobile interstitials that block content will tank rankings.

✗ Not optimizing for real mobile behavior

→ Are your CTAs visible without scrolling? Can people find what they need in 5 seconds?

Mobile Navigation: Simpler is Better

Navigation should feel intuitive and lightning fast.

- Use a hamburger menu that's easy to open
- Limit menu items to the essentials
- Use sticky headers carefully (don't block half the screen)
- Test drop-downs and accordions—are they smooth on all devices?

Use Hotjar or Microsoft Clarity session
recordings to watch how real people use
your mobile site. You'll spot friction
in seconds.

Mini Exercise: Mobile UX Reality Check

Grab your phone and test your own site (or a client's):

1. Open homepage, product page, and blog post
2. Try to buy something, find contact info, or read a guide
3. Ask yourself:
   - Is this experience smooth, fast, and frustration-free?
   - Would *I* stay on this site?
   - What would annoy a non-techy user?

Fix 2–3 pain points immediately: size up buttons, simplify menu, reduce load time.

Checklist: Mobile Optimization Done Right

- Site loads in under 3s on 4G
- Mobile version has all the same content as desktop
- Text and buttons are large enough to tap without zoom
- Navigation is simple and thumb-friendly
- No layout shifts, overlapping elements, or hidden content
- Forms are easy to use on mobile
- No full-screen popups
- Tested on multiple devices and screen sizes

Recap: Mobile-First, Not Mobile-After

- Google prioritizes your mobile version for rankings
- Responsive isn't enough—optimize for real mobile behavior
- Speed, simplicity, and usability rule
- If mobile sucks, so does your SEO. Fix it before worrying about anything else.

Coming Up Next:

Now that your mobile game is solid, let's make sure Google can actually find and index your pages. In Chapter 10, we'll talk about Crawlability and Indexability—how to make your site as accessible to bots as it is to humans.

Chapter 10: Crawlability and Indexability – Getting Google to See Your Site

You could have the best content in the world... but if Google can't crawl and index it, it's invisible.

SEO isn't just about keywords, backlinks, and content. At its core, it's about visibility—and that starts with making sure search engines can crawl your pages, understand them, and index them properly.

If you've ever wondered:

- Why isn't this page showing up in Google?
- Why is my blog post indexed, but not ranking?
- Why do I have 10,000 indexed URLs and only 3 clicks?

This chapter is for you.

Crawling vs. Indexing: What's the Difference?

These two terms often get confused, but they're not the same.

Crawling

This is when Googlebot (Google's crawler) *visits* your website and scans the pages. It follows links, reads your HTML, and collects data.

Indexing

Once crawled, Google decides whether to *store* the page in its index. If a page isn't indexed, it won't show up in search results—ever.

 Think of crawling as getting noticed, and indexing as getting remembered. You need both for SEO to work.

Make Sure Googlebot Can Access Your Site

The very first step: don't accidentally block the bot.

Check your:

1. Robots.txt File

Located at yourdomain.com/robots.txt

Make sure you're not disallowing key pages or entire folders.

Good:
```
User-agent: *
Disallow: /cart/
Disallow: /checkout/
```

Bad:
```
User-agent: *
Disallow: /
```

(That blocks everything!)

2. Meta Robots Tags

You can set individual pages to noindex, which tells Google not to index them.

That's great for:

- Thank-you pages
- Internal search results
- Staging/duplicate content
- Admin pages

But it's a disaster if you accidentally noindex your homepage or blog.

Use noindex sparingly and intentionally.

Your Sitemap: Google's Roadmap

A sitemap is a file (usually XML) that lists the pages you want Google to crawl and index.

Most CMS platforms generate one automatically:

- Shopify: yourstore.com/sitemap.xml
- Webflow: same
- WordPress: use SEO plugins like RankMath or Yoast

Submit it to Google Search Console > Sitemaps

Make sure it only includes:

- Index-worthy pages (no thank-you, cart, filters)

- Canonical versions of each URL

Canonical Tags: Solving Duplicate Content Issues

If multiple pages have similar content (like product variations or filter pages), use a canonical tag to tell Google which one is the "main" version.

This prevents Google from:

- Thinking your site is spammy
- Wasting crawl budget
- Splitting ranking signals across duplicates

 Don't canonically link every page to the homepage. That's like telling Google "ignore this, look over there" on every page. Only use canonicals when there's real duplication.

Fix Crawl Errors (Regularly!)

In Google Search Console, check the Pages report (under "Indexing") to see:

- Pages that *aren't indexed* (and why)
- Server errors (5xx)
- Redirect chains or loops
- Pages blocked by robots.txt or marked noindex

Fix what's broken, especially if:

- It's a key page
- You want it to rank
- It's part of a user journey (like checkout or contact)

Don't Waste Crawl Budget

Google doesn't crawl every site the same way. Sites with more traffic, better structure, and clean internal links get crawled more often and more deeply.

Here's how to avoid wasting crawl budget:

- Avoid infinite scroll or endless filters that create thousands of URLs
- Don't index thin, low-value pages
- Remove or block duplicate content

- Improve your internal linking structure (remember Chapter 7?)

Mini Exercise: Index Check + Robots Audit

1. Google this:

   site:yourdomain.com

   → See what pages are indexed (are there surprises?)

2. Go to Search Console > Indexing > Pages

   → Check "Why pages aren't indexed"

3. Check your robots.txt at yourdomain.com/robots.txt

   → Are you blocking anything important?

4. Open a few core pages and view source

   → Look for (should NOT be there unless intentional)

Checklist: Crawlability & Indexability Audit

- Sitemap is submitted and includes all key pages
- No key pages are blocked in robots.txt
- No accidental noindex tags

- Canonical tags are used correctly (and sparingly)
- Crawl errors in Search Console are resolved
- Duplicate/thin pages are handled properly
- Internal linking supports crawl paths
- You've done a "site:" search and reviewed indexed pages

Recap: If Google Can't See It, It Doesn't Exist

- Crawling = getting discovered
- Indexing = getting stored
- Schema, speed, and links are useless if the page isn't in the index
- Tools like Search Console help you stay on top of issues

Coming Up Next:

In Chapter 11, we'll walk through the wild world of Google Algorithm Updates—what they are, how they work, and what to do when they hit.

Chapter 11: Understanding Google Algorithm Updates

Because one day, you'll wake up and your traffic will be gone. Here's how to avoid that.

Google is constantly updating how it ranks websites—sometimes with small tweaks, sometimes with massive overhauls that flip rankings overnight. If you've ever felt like your traffic dropped "for no reason," chances are, an algorithm update was behind it.

Understanding how updates work (and how to respond to them) is what separates amateurs from SEO pros.

Types of Google Algorithm Updates

There are two broad categories:

1. Core Updates

- These happen a few times per year (typically 3–5)
- Broad changes to how Google assesses content, intent, and authority
- Sites gain or lose rankings *sitewide*—not just on one page

2. Targeted Updates

- Focused on a specific area, like:
    - Spam (SpamBrain)
    - Page Experience (Core Web Vitals)
    - Reviews (Product Reviews Update)
    - Helpful Content
- These updates are often stealthy and affect only specific types of sites or industries

The worst thing you can do after an update is panic and "SEO harder." Updates reward consistency, not overreaction.

A Quick History of Major Updates

Here's a crash course in the big ones:

Update	What It Targeted
Panda (2011)	Thin, low-quality content
Penguin (2012)	Spammy backlinks, keyword stuffing
Hummingbird (2013)	User intent and conversational queries
RankBrain (2015)	AI-assisted query interpretation
Medic (2018)	YMYL (Your Money Your Life) content
BERT (2019)	Natural language understanding
Core Web Vitals (2021+)	Page speed, UX, layout shifts

Helpful Content (2022+)	AI junk, unhelpful content, sitewide value check
Spam Updates (ongoing)	Cloaking, spammy links, fake content

Knowing these helps you understand what went wrong when traffic dips.

How to Know If You've Been Hit

Signs of an update hit:

- Sharp drop in organic traffic (especially across *many* pages)
- Pages ranking on page 1 suddenly vanish or fall to page 5+
- Search Console impressions tank, but your content hasn't changed

Check tools like:

- Google Search Status Dashboard
- Moz Algorithm History
- Semrush Sensor

- RankRanger Google Updates Tool

If your drop aligns with one of these updates—*you've been hit.*

```
Don't confuse algorithm updates with
technical issues. Always check for
crawling errors, broken redirects, or
deindexed pages before blaming Google.
```

How to Recover From an Algorithm Hit

Recovery starts with a brutally honest audit. Google doesn't punish—it re-evaluates. Here's what to do:

1. Analyze Which Pages Dropped

- Use Search Console to identify pages with the biggest traffic dips
- Are they thin? Outdated? Not helpful?

2. Check Your Content Quality

- Is it written by someone with real experience?

- Does it satisfy user intent *better* than top-ranking results?
- Is it genuinely helpful—or written for Google?

3. Improve E-E-A-T

- Add author bios, external citations, trust signals
- Clean up grammar, clarity, and structure
- Remove fluff, add substance

4. Strengthen Internal Links

- Guide Google to your most important content
- Update anchor text and relevance

5. Clean Your Link Profile

- Disavow spammy backlinks if needed (rare, but possible)
- Focus on earning legit links from real sites

Never start rewriting everything in a panic. If one part of your site dropped, don't torch the rest. Find patterns before making changes.

How to Future-Proof Your Site

You can't predict every update—but you can build resilience into your SEO:

- Focus on topic authority, not one-hit wonders
- Refresh content every few months
- Diversify your traffic (email, social, direct—not just SEO)
- Avoid black-hat tactics, AI content farms, or paid link schemes
- Build a brand, not just a blog

If your site becomes a trusted destination, you'll survive most updates—and thrive in the long run.

Mini Exercise: Update Immunity Scorecard

Rate yourself (1–5) on the following:

- My content is written by real people with real experience
- Each post satisfies a clear user intent
- I update top pages regularly
- I have strong internal linking between related content
- I've checked for technical issues in Search Console
- I know which updates have affected my industry

- My site builds trust (real business info, contact, terms, author pages)

A score under 20? Time to reinforce.

Checklist: Surviving and Thriving Through Updates

- Track algorithm history and industry-specific changes
- Audit content for E-E-A-T and helpfulness
- Use Search Console and analytics to monitor traffic dips
- Fix thin, outdated, or misleading pages
- Strengthen topical depth and internal linking
- Focus on user experience, not search engine tricks
- Think long-term: build trust and authority

Recap: Don't Just React. Adapt.

- Updates aren't punishments—they're recalibrations
- If you got hit, something wasn't working
- Focus on quality, clarity, experience, and value
- SEO is a long game. Play to win it, not just survive the next shake-up.

Coming Up Next:

We're heading into Off-Page SEO next—starting with Backlinks: The Currency of SEO. If content is your voice, backlinks are your reputation. Let's learn how to earn the ones that matter.

Chapter 12: Backlinks – The Currency of SEO

Content is your voice. Backlinks are your reputation.

Backlinks Are Like Getting Introduced at a Party

Let's make this simple:

Imagine walking into a crowded party where no one knows who you are. You could shout "I'm awesome!" and hope someone believes you—or someone could walk over, tap a few shoulders, and say:

"Hey, you should meet her—she really knows her stuff about [furniture design / copywriting / whatever you do]."

That's a high-quality backlink.
The *person introducing you* is the linking website.
Their reputation matters—if it's someone everyone respects, your credibility skyrockets.
If it's someone shady in a trench coat whispering in the corner? Not so helpful.

The more respected sites that introduce you, the more people (and Google) start to listen.

In Google's eyes, a backlink is a vote of confidence—someone else pointing to your site and saying, "This content is worth linking to." But not all votes are equal.

Backlinks from trusted, relevant sites = SEO gold.
Backlinks from spammy, unrelated sites = SEO poison.

This chapter is about earning the right kind of links, avoiding the bad ones, and building a backlink profile that screams *authority*.

What Makes a Backlink Valuable?

Let's break it down:

Relevance

The linking site should be related to your niche.
A link from a home decor blog to your furniture site? Great.
A link from a sketchy casino blog? Not so much.

Authority

The higher the Domain Authority (DA) or Domain Rating (DR) of the linking site, the more powerful the link.

- A single link from The Guardian might outweigh 50 from random blogs.

- Use tools like Ahrefs, Moz, or Semrush to check DR/DA.

Trust

Was the link earned organically? Does it sit in high-quality content?
Is the site known for real editorial work—or just selling links?

Anchor Text

The clickable text matters.
Natural > over-optimized.
"See our coffee table guide" is better than "cheap oak coffee tables UK" 14 times in a row.

```
Backlinks are like dating: you want
quality, mutual respect, and someone
who's not toxic. The rest? Not worth it.
```

Backlink Myths You Should Ignore

✘ "More is better"

Nope. 10 high-quality backlinks > 100 low-quality junk links.

✖ "Only homepage links matter"

Internal pages need love too—especially blog posts and product/category pages.

✖ "Any backlink helps"

If it's from a spammy site, in a footer farm, or clearly paid—it can hurt you.

The Fiverr Trap: "300 Backlinks for $5" Will Ruin You

It sounds tempting. You're new to SEO, and someone's offering hundreds of backlinks for the price of a coffee. It feels like a shortcut to instant Google love.

But what you're actually buying is:

- Spammy blog comments on irrelevant forums
- Junk directories that exist only to manipulate search rankings
- Foreign PBNs (Private Blog Networks) that Google's already flagged

At best, these links do nothing. At worst, they put your site on Google's naughty list.

Here's what usually happens:

- You buy the package, see 200+ links show up.
- Everything seems fine for a while.
- Two or three months later, your traffic tanks.
- Google's algorithm catches up and starts devaluing your site.
- Recovery takes *months*, even if you disavow the bad links.

Moral of the story: If a backlink deal feels too good to be true, it is.

So How Do You Get Good Backlinks—For Free?

The good news: real backlinks are free. But they're not effortless.

Let's start with the two easiest, most effective beginner-friendly methods: directories and guest posting.

1. **Local and Niche Directories** (Low Effort, High Value)

This is your starting point. Submitting your business to trusted directories is boring work—but it builds a strong, clean backlink profile early on.

Benefits:

- You get backlinks from aged, high-domain authority sites.
- You increase your local visibility and get referral traffic.
- You create NAP consistency (Name, Address, Phone), which helps with local SEO.

Example directories:

- Yell.com
- Thomson Local
- FreeIndex
- Hotfrog
- Manta
- UK Small Business Directory
- Cylex
- Local Chamber of Commerce listings

Yes, you'll have to paste your business info and description again and again. But this isn't just for SEO—it's how customers and Google find and trust you.

2. **Guest Posting** (Smart, Scalable, and Long-Term)

Once you've done your keyword research, started producing content, and understand EEAT principles—it's time to share your expertise on *other people's websites.*

Most blog owners are looking for:

- Fresh, quality content
- Industry experts
- Real contributors who bring insight

They usually offer:

- A link in your author bio
- A contextual link inside the article itself

Both are valuable:

- Author bio builds your personal brand and signals authorship to Google.
- Contextual link (e.g., linking to your blog post or product page) passes SEO authority directly to your site.

How to Find Guest Posting Opportunities

It's way easier than people think.

Just type this into Google:

```
"Write for us" + [your niche]
```

Examples:

```
"Write for us" + marketing

"Write for us" + pets

"Write for us" + real estate

"Write for us" + mental health
```

Google will give you a list of blogs, media sites, and communities that accept contributions in your niche.

What to Look For Before You Pitch

Not all guest posting offers are created equal. Before you send an email or draft an article, check for:

- **Do-follow link policy:** Do they allow real links or only "nofollow"?
- **Author bio options:** Can you link to your homepage or social?
- **Domain authority and traffic:** Use Ahrefs or SimilarWeb to see if the site gets actual visitors.
- **Topic fit:** Will their readers care about your topic?

Some huge platforms like Entrepreneur, Forbes, or Inc. might ask for a fee—or take months to reply. Don't be discouraged. Focus on mid-tier, topic-specific sites where your voice adds real value.

What to Write and Where to Link

Write content that:

- Solves a real problem
- Aligns with the site's audience
- Naturally links to your best article or landing page

Example:

Let's say you run a dog training site.

Guest post idea:

"5 Mistakes First-Time Dog Owners Make (and How to Fix Them)"

Natural link in the article:

"…use consistent commands like those in this dog obedience checklist…"

The link feels useful—not forced. That's key.

Bonus Free Backlink Tactics You Can Start Today

1. Journalist Platforms

Journalists post daily queries for expert quotes. If you reply and get quoted, you get a backlink from major news outlets like Business Insider, Mashable, etc.

There was a very popular platform called HARO (Help a Reporter Out), which is now closed. But there are plenty of alternatives with the same principle.

- Sign up
- Check relevant categories that reflect your niche

- Get email notifications about relevant topics that journalists needs help with
- Respond fast, and write clearly—journalists are busy

2. Link Roundups

Some bloggers post weekly or monthly "best of" content roundups.

Search Google for:

```
"[your niche] link roundup"
"best articles this week" + [niche]
"monthly resources" + [topic]
```

Find a few, then pitch them your best article.

3. Broken Link Building

Use a tool like Ahrefs or Check My Links (Chrome extension) to find broken outbound links on related sites. Email the site owner and suggest your content as a replacement.

4. Testimonials and Case Studies

Write short testimonials for tools or services you use (e.g., Ahrefs, SEMrush, Canva). Companies often showcase them—with a backlink.

5. Share Your Content in Niche Forums or Communities

Sites like Reddit, Quora, Indie Hackers, or industry-specific forums are great for building early backlinks (especially if you're genuinely helpful, not salesy).

Don't spam—engage, add value, and link where appropriate.

```
Use Ahrefs → Content Explorer → search
your topic → filter by referring
domains
That's how you find content that already
earns backlinks.
```

How to Do Outreach Without Sounding Like a Robot

Bad outreach kills good content. Here's how to not be that person:

- Personalize your email: mention their site, article, or work
- Be direct: "I wrote this piece on [topic]—thought it could add value to your article on [X]."

- Don't fake flattery: "Big fan" means nothing if you've clearly never read their site
- Follow up once, not seven times

If your content is genuinely good, one email is often enough.

Spotting and Avoiding Toxic Backlinks

Use Ahrefs or Google Search Console to audit your backlinks. Watch out for:

- Links from PBNs (private blog networks)
- Sites with 0 traffic and hundreds of outbound links
- Foreign-language spam sites
- Links in irrelevant comments or footers

If you find them:

- Ask for removal (good luck)
- Use Google's Disavow Tool (carefully)

But don't panic—Google's algorithms are good at ignoring trash links unless you're actively spamming.

Mini Exercise: Analyze Your Backlink Profile

1. Open Ahrefs / Moz / Search Console → Check your

    backlink list

2. Sort by:
    - Domain authority (DR/DA)
    - Referring domains
    - Anchors
3. Ask:
    - Do these links come from real, relevant sites?
    - Do I have too many exact-match anchors?
    - Which pages have no links at all?
4. Make a hitlist of 5 pages you want to build links to.

Checklist: A Healthy Backlink Profile

- Links come from relevant and trusted sources
- Mix of homepage, product, blog, and category links
- Anchor text is diverse and natural
- No spammy, toxic, or paid link patterns
- You're consistently earning—not buying—links
- At least a few *linkable assets* are live on your site
- Outreach is happening monthly or quarterly

Recap: Your Reputation Is Built Off-Page

- Backlinks are still the #1 ranking factor outside your content
- Focus on *quality over quantity*
- Build content worth linking to, then tell people about it
- Stay clean. Stay relevant. Stay useful.

Coming Up Next:

Next up: Local SEO and Citations—because if you're a local business and you're not ranking on Maps, you're leaving money on the table.

Chapter 13: Local SEO and Citations – Own Your Area

You don't need to be #1 globally. Just be the first name locals see when they search.

Local SEO is a game-changer for brick-and-mortar stores, service providers, and even online businesses with regional focus. Why?

Because people aren't just searching "furniture."
They're searching "furniture store near me" or "custom wardrobes Leeds."

And if you're not in the Local 3-Pack (that little Google Maps box above all the regular search results)? You're missing the hottest traffic there is.

Why Local SEO Matters

- 46% of all Google searches are local
- 76% of people who search for something nearby visit a business within a day
- 28% of local searches result in a purchase

So yeah, being visible locally isn't a "nice to have." It's survival.

Start With Your Google Business Profile (GBP)

Your Google Business Profile (formerly Google My Business) is your *home base* for local SEO.

Set it up at google.com/business

Key elements to fill out:

- Business name (must match your signage/site EXACTLY)
- Address (or service area if you don't have a storefront)
- Phone number (local, not 0800 if possible)
- Website URL
- Opening hours (and holiday updates)
- Business category (choose the closest match)
- Description (focus on keywords + unique selling points)
- Photos (real ones, not just logos—exterior, interior, staff, products)

Add FAQs and posts to your GBP
regularly. It shows Google you're active
—and gives potential customers more
reasons to choose you.

NAP Consistency: It's Not Just Boring Admin

NAP stands for Name, Address and Phone number.
It must be consistent across every platform—your website,
directories, social media, and GBP.

Why? Because Google cross-checks it. Inconsistencies (like
"St." vs "Street" or different phone numbers) weaken trust.

Check your NAP consistency using:

- BrightLocal's Citation Tracker
- Whitespark
- Manual Google search: "Your Business Name" +
  "Address" and check what shows up

Local Citations: Digital Mentions That Matter

A citation is any online mention of your business's NAP info. Think:

- Yelp
- Yell
- Facebook
- Apple Maps
- Trustpilot
- Hotfrog
- Local chamber of commerce sites

Citations help build trust and reinforce your local presence.

You don't need 500—just high-quality, industry-relevant, and region-specific ones.

Don't fall for "we'll build 300 local citations for $5" spam. Most of those links go to junk directories that nobody visits—and Google ignores (or penalizes).

Get Reviews (And Respond to Them!)

Reviews don't just convert customers—they influence rankings.

- Ask every happy customer to leave a review on Google
- Automate it via email/text follow-ups or post-purchase flows
- Always reply (even to bad reviews) politely and helpfully
- Use relevant keywords naturally in your responses (e.g., "Thanks for your feedback on our custom dining tables!")

Other review sites like Trustpilot, Facebook, or industry-specific platforms also help—but Google is king.

Local Landing Pages: Don't Just Rely on Maps

If you serve multiple areas, create location-specific landing pages.

Example:
/custom-kitchens-london

/custom-kitchens-washington

/custom-kitchens-tokyo

Each page should:

- Include location in H1, title, meta description, URL
- Mention the city in context (not just keyword stuffing)
- Include a map or embedded GBP
- Highlight local projects, testimonials, or service areas

Mini Exercise: Local SEO Quick Wins

1. Search "your service + your city"

   → Are you in the 3-pack? Are you even on page 1?

2. Google your business name

   → Are your NAP details consistent across all results?

3. Check your Google Business Profile

   → Does it have:
   - Description
   - Hours
   - Recent posts
   - At least 10+ good reviews?
4. Make a list of 10 citation sites to update or submit to

Checklist: Local SEO Essentials

- Google Business Profile fully optimized and verified
- NAP is 100% consistent across all platforms
- 10–30 quality citations set up and correct
- At least 10 recent Google reviews (and growing)
- Unique local landing pages for each service area
- Respond to all reviews (positive and negative)
- Regular GBP posts and photo uploads
- Mobile-friendly, fast-loading local pages

Recap: Be the Local Obvious Choice

- Optimize your Google Business Profile—it's your storefront
- Keep your NAP consistent and clean
- Build trust through reviews and citations
- Create landing pages that feel hyper-local
- Show up *where* and *when* people need you

Coming Up Next:
In Chapter 14, we'll explore Social Signals and Brand Mentions—a subtle but powerful way to reinforce your SEO

through visibility, even if it doesn't always show up in a direct ranking factor list.

Chapter 14: Social Signals and Brand Mentions – SEO's Silent Influencers

You might not rank from a like or a share... but the ripple effect is real.

In the SEO world, there's this long-running debate:

"Do social signals help rankings?"

Technically? No.
But practically? Absolutely yes.

Not because Google says, "Oh, 50 likes, let's rank it higher," but because social activity drives visibility, builds brand awareness, and generates links and mentions—which *do* affect rankings.

What Are Social Signals, Anyway?

Social signals are actions like:

- Likes
- Shares
- Comments

- Follows
- Saves
- Retweets
- Tags

  ...basically, all the ways people interact with your content on platforms like Instagram, TikTok, LinkedIn, Facebook, and Twitter/X.

And while Google doesn't directly count them as ranking factors, social signals:

- Increase content exposure
- Get your brand and links in front of new people
- Trigger brand searches (which *are* SEO signals)
- Lead to backlinks and citations over time

 Social media is your distribution engine. If you build great content and no one sees it—did it even exist?

Why Brand Mentions Matter for SEO

Google is smart enough to understand implied links—also known as unlinked brand mentions.

Let's say someone writes:

"I just bought a custom wardrobe from Oak & Iron and the craftsmanship is insane."

There's no link.
But Google *sees* the brand name, the context, and the sentiment.

These kinds of mentions:

- Reinforce E-E-A-T (Experience, Expertise, Authoritativeness, Trust)
- Strengthen your entity profile (Google's internal understanding of your brand)
- Often lead to real backlinks later

How to Build Social SEO Without Being Cringe

You don't need to go viral or dance on TikTok—just build trust and visibility.

Focus on:

- Sharing your best content (guides, tools, data, before/after)
- Engaging with comments (even 5 mins a day goes a long way)
- Partnering with micro-influencers in your niche
- Creating shareable visuals (infographics, carousels, cheat sheets)
- Answering questions in Facebook groups or Reddit threads with value—not spam

 Add social share buttons to your blog posts and product pages. Make it easy for people to share what they like.

Monitor Your Brand Like a Pro

Track when and where your brand is mentioned—even without a link.

Tools to use:

- Google Alerts – set up alerts for your brand, product names, or slogans
- Brand24 or Mention – more advanced tracking, sentiment analysis
- Semrush Brand Monitoring Tool – shows new and lost mentions
- Ahrefs Content Explorer – find where your brand appears in content

If you find a mention without a link?
Politely reach out and ask for one. You'd be surprised how often it works.

Mini Exercise: Brand Visibility Pulse Check

1. Google your brand name

   → What shows up? Are the top results accurate and

   branded?

2. Set up a Google Alert for:
   - Your brand name
   - Your product names
   - Your slogan or hashtag

3. Choose 1 post or page from your site and create 3

   social media captions promoting it.

→ One for Instagram, one for LinkedIn, and one for Facebook/Twitter

4. Post it. Track shares, comments, and link clicks.

Checklist: Social and Brand SEO Health

- Brand name is consistent across all platforms
- Social profiles link back to your site
- You're regularly sharing your best content
- You respond to comments and engage with your audience
- You monitor brand mentions and link opportunities
- Social share buttons are on key pages
- At least 1–2 influencer or community collabs per quarter
- You've Googled your brand name in the past 30 days

Recap: You Can't Be Found If No One Knows You Exist

- Social signals amplify your content
- Brand mentions strengthen trust and entity recognition

- Visibility leads to links, links lead to rankings
- You don't need to be viral—just visible and consistent

Coming Up Next:
We're entering Advanced SEO Strategies, starting with Content Optimization and Refreshing—because sometimes, your next big win isn't creating new content... it's updating the gold you already have.

Chapter 15: Content Optimization and Refreshing – Breathe New Life Into Old Gold

Sometimes your next SEO win is already on your site—just a little dusty.

Most websites are sitting on a goldmine of underperforming content—blog posts, service pages, guides, or category descriptions that are good... but not great. They rank on page 2 or 3, get a trickle of traffic, and are forgotten.

But here's the thing:
It's way easier to boost an existing piece of content from page 2 to page 1 than it is to create something brand new and make it rank.

This chapter is about auditing, optimizing, and refreshing content to unlock fast wins and long-term growth.

SEO Isn't "Set and Forget"

You might assume that once a blog post or landing page is live, your job is done. But in reality, content has a shelf life. It can age, lose relevance, slip in rankings, or get overtaken by fresher, better content.

Google wants to serve the most current, helpful results. And if your content looks neglected—or worse, outdated—you'll slowly drop off the radar.

What Is Content Decay?

Content decay is the gradual decline in organic traffic and visibility of previously high-performing content.

You've probably seen it before:

- A blog post that used to bring in 1,000+ visits a month now gets 150
- A how-to guide that ranked #3 now floats somewhere on page 5
- An article you haven't touched in two years is outranked by copycat posts that are newer

This isn't just a traffic problem—it's a brand trust problem too.

Content decay visualisation

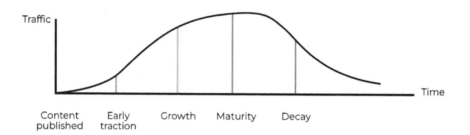

Traffic

Time

Content published | Early traction | Growth | Maturity | Decay

Why Content Decays Over Time

1. **Search intent evolves**
   What users wanted 18 months ago might not be what they want today.
2. **New competitors enter the SERPs**
   Your old post may be outperformed by a newer, richer, more optimized article.
3. **Outdated information**
   Broken links, old stats, or discontinued tools turn readers (and Google) off.

4. **Thin or vague content**
   A post that once passed as "helpful" now gets penalized for lack of depth.
5. **Technical or structural issues**
   If the page becomes slow, broken, or unlinked from your nav, it stops getting crawled.

Think of it like a wardrobe: you don't need more clothes—you just need to style the good pieces better and donate the outdated ones.

The Content Optimization Process (Step-by-Step)

Let's make this practical. Here's how to turn underperforming content into SEO gold:

Step 1: Identify Declining Pages

Use tools like:

- **Google Search Console** → Compare past 3 months vs. previous 3

- **Ahrefs / SEMrush / Ubersuggest** → Track drops in traffic, position, backlinks

- **Google Analytics** → Spot high-bounce or low-engagement pages

Flag any content that has:

- Dropped in ranking or impressions
- Lost clicks over time
- Stagnated in position despite optimization

Step 2: Understand Why It's Declining

Ask:

- Does this still match current search intent?
- Is the info still accurate?
- How does it compare to the top 3 current results?
- Can it be merged with another post for better authority?

Use a fresh Google search for the keyword—study what's ranking now. What formats, lengths, and angles do the top pages use?

Step 3: Optimize & Refresh

Here's what you might do:

- Update outdated data, examples, and screenshots
- Add new sections to increase depth
- Insert internal links to newer articles
- Improve formatting and readability
- Add a table of contents or jump links
- Update meta title & description for higher click-through
- Re-upload images in modern formats (WebP)
- Ensure it passes Core Web Vitals audits

Pro tip: Don't rewrite everything. Just enhance what's already working.

Step 4: Re-index & Track

Once your updates are live:

- Re-submit the URL in Google Search Console

- Track rankings over the next 2–6 weeks
- Compare click and impression trends

If your content was stuck for months and suddenly moves up—*you'll know the update worked.*

When to Redirect or Merge Content

Not every piece is worth saving. If you've got:

- Multiple short articles targeting the same topic
- Posts with low-quality backlinks or thin content
- Duplicates of a better-performing version

Then the better play might be to merge them into one superpage—or 301 redirect the weak content to a stronger parent post.

This consolidates authority, improves structure, and avoids keyword cannibalization.

Set Up a Content Refresh Calendar

Don't rely on memory. Build a quarterly or biannual refresh routine:

- Prioritize content that's already performing well (but slipping)
- Track last updated dates in your CMS or Notion board
- Make sure cornerstone pages never go 12+ months without a touch-up

Final Tip: Think "Content Assets", Not "Blog Posts"

When you treat content like an asset, you maintain it, not just publish and forget it. Great SEO content compounds over time—but only if you give it the attention it deserves.

Mini Exercise: Find Your Low-Hanging Fruit

1. Open Google Search Console → Performance → Pages
2. Filter for pages with avg. position between 11–30
3. Pick 1 blog post or page with potential
4. Update the intro, add one section, improve title/meta, and republish
5. Watch what happens over the next 30 days

Checklist: Content Refresh Ready

- Audit performed using GSC / Analytics / SEO tools
- Outdated content updated or removed
- New stats, visuals, or examples added
- Keywords refined for intent and structure
- Internal links added
- Meta title and description rewritten
- Schema applied
- Page republished and re-promoted
- Results monitored in 2–4 weeks

Recap: Don't Let Good Content Rot

- You already did 80% of the work—make it 100%
- Updated content = higher rankings + better user experience
- Refresh > rewrite
- The fastest SEO wins are often already on your site

Bonus: Signs It's Time to Refresh a Page or Post

Declining Performance

- Traffic to the page has dropped over the past few months
- Rankings have slipped from page 1 to page 2 or lower
- Click-through rate (CTR) is low despite good impressions

Outdated Information

- Stats, tools, or examples are more than a year old
- You've mentioned dates or years that are now outdated (e.g., "Top Trends for 2022")
- The industry or topic has evolved and your content hasn't

Missing Search Intent

- The page no longer aligns with what users are looking for
- Your competitors' newer content is answering the query better
- The format is wrong (you wrote a blog when people want a comparison chart, guide, or FAQ)

Low Engagement

- High bounce rate
- Low average time on page
- Few internal links leading *to* or *from* it

- It's not earning backlinks or shares

Technical or SEO Issues

- Meta title/description are weak, outdated, or missing
- No schema markup is applied
- Thin content (less than 500 words)
- Content structure is messy or hard to scan

Just... Forgotten

- You haven't touched the post/page since you published it
- It's buried deep in your blog/archive
- You've created new, better content—but haven't linked it here
- You've learned a lot since then, and your tone or quality has improved

If your content ticks 2–3 of these boxes, it's time for a refresh. If it ticks 5+, than... don't just update it. Overhaul it.

Coming Up Next:
In Chapter 16, we're diving into Voice Search and Featured Snippets—because the future of SEO isn't just about clicks. Sometimes, the best position... is zero.

Chapter 16: Voice Search and Featured Snippets – Targeting Position Zero

SEO isn't just about ranking anymore. It's about being the answer.

The way people search is changing.

We don't just type keywords anymore—we talk to our phones, ask Siri questions in the car, or shout across the kitchen at Alexa. These queries are longer, more conversational, and often lead to a single answer being read aloud.

At the same time, Google has introduced featured snippets— the "Position Zero" results that appear *above* the first result, pulling a block of text directly into the SERPs.

This chapter is about how to optimize for both, and claim more visibility—even when no one clicks.

What Is Voice Search (and Why It Matters)

Voice search is what happens when users speak instead of type:

- "What's the best wood for dining tables?"
- "How long does shipping take for Oak & Iron?"
- "Where can I buy affordable office chairs near me?"

These queries tend to be:

- Longer (6–10 words)
- Conversational
- Question-based
- Intent-heavy (people want quick answers, now)

If your content isn't structured to answer questions clearly and fast—you're out of the running.

What Is a Featured Snippet?

A featured snippet is the box that appears at the top of Google's search results. It answers a query directly, pulled from a webpage.

Common formats:

- Paragraphs (most common)
- Lists (step-by-step, how-tos)
- Tables
- Videos (sometimes YouTube)

You've probably seen them as:

"What is Schema Markup?"

Snippet appears with a short explanation and link to the source.

These snippets often power voice search results too.

 If Google chooses your answer to show before all other results, you've already won—even if users don't click.

How to Optimize for Voice Search

1. Answer specific questions
    o   Use headings like "What is...", "How does...", "Can I..."
    o   Write in a clear, natural tone—avoid jargon
2. Use long-tail conversational keywords
    o   Think: "best chair for lower back pain" vs. "ergonomic chair"
    o   Tools: AlsoAsked, AnswerThePublic, Semrush's Questions tab
3. Include FAQs on key pages
    o   Use question-answer format (and mark up with FAQ schema)

- Answer in 2–4 sentence blocks
4. Aim for brevity in answers
    - Voice search snippets are short—try to answer in under 50 words
    - Then expand below for detail (both formats win)
5. Be mobile- and speed-optimized
    - Voice users are often on phones, in a rush
    - Slow sites or confusing UX don't convert

How to Win Featured Snippets

Google pulls snippets from pages that:

- Are already ranking in the top 10
- Structure content clearly (headings, lists, tables)
- Directly answer specific questions

Tips to win:

- Use subheadings with question phrasing
- Immediately answer the question in 1–2 sentences
- Use clean HTML, clear formatting
- Add bulleted or numbered lists for step-by-step content
- Break large topics into scannable sections

Example:
H2: How to Clean a Wooden Dining Table

Paragraph: To clean a wooden dining table, use a soft cloth and a mild soap solution. Avoid excess water. Wipe dry immediately with a clean towel.

Bullet List (optional):

- Dust with soft cloth
- Use mild soap and water
- Dry thoroughly

 You can't "force" a snippet, but you can make your content the easiest and clearest option. Google will reward that.

Mini Exercise: Snippet Sniping

1. Pick a question your audience asks (e.g. "What size dining table seats 6 people?")
2. Google it—see if a featured snippet exists
3. If yes:
    - Study how it's formatted
    - Can you create a better, clearer version?
4. If no:

- That's an opportunity—create a short answer block and post it on a blog or FAQ page

Checklist: Voice Search and Snippet Readiness

- You target long-tail and question-based keywords
- Your content includes short, direct answer blocks
- H2/H3 headers are phrased as questions
- You use lists or tables where useful
- Pages are mobile- and speed-optimized
- FAQ sections are marked with schema
- You've reviewed existing snippets and aimed to improve on them
- Your content reads naturally and sounds good when spoken aloud

Recap: Think Like a Human, Speak Like a Search Result

- Voice and featured snippets reward clear, helpful, fast answers
- Structure and brevity matter more than ever
- Aim to be the result that answers *before* the click
- If you do it right, Google does the heavy lifting—and you win visibility

Coming Up Next:

Next chapter: International SEO — perfect if you're targeting multiple countries, languages, or want to grow beyond your local market.

Chapter 17: International SEO – Going Global Without Losing Your Rankings

Because Google doesn't care what language you speak—unless you tell it clearly.

Expanding your website to new languages or countries sounds exciting—until your traffic tanks because Google doesn't know which version of your site to show where.

This chapter is about proper international SEO setup: language targeting, hreflang tags, localization, and choosing the right domain structure so each audience gets the version that fits them best.

When Do You Need International SEO?

If any of these apply to you, this chapter is for you:

- You sell in or serve multiple countries
- You have customers who speak different languages
- You've created duplicate sites for each region (but they're not ranking well)

- You want to dominate local search *and* international visibility

International SEO isn't just translating text—it's sending Google clear, technical signals about which version is for whom.

Step 1: Choose Your International Site Structure

There are three main approaches:

1. **Country-Code Top-Level Domains** (ccTLDs)

Example: example.co.uk, example.de, example.fr

Pros:

- Strong geo-targeting
- Easy for users to trust

Cons:

- Expensive to maintain
- Harder to consolidate domain authority

2. **Subdirectories**

Example: example.com/uk/, example.com/fr/

Pros:

- Shares domain authority
- Easy to manage in one CMS

Cons:

- Slightly weaker location signal to Google (but still very effective with hreflang)

3. **Subdomains**

Example: uk.example.com, fr.example.com

Pros:

- Can separate content/platforms easily
- More flexible

Cons:

- Treated almost like separate sites (need individual SEO work)

 Unless there's a strong reason to do otherwise, subdirectories are often the best balance of SEO power and simplicity.

Step 2: Use Hreflang Tags Correctly

The magic tag of international SEO: hreflang

It tells Google:

"This page is the English version for the UK."
"This other one is the Spanish version for Spain."

Without it, Google might:

- Index the wrong version in the wrong country
- See your translations as duplicate content
- Confuse users with the wrong language

Each version of a page should reference every other version—including itself.
Keep the x-default tag for generic/global versions.

Tools to help:

- Ahrefs Site Audit
- Screaming Frog
- Merkle Hreflang Generator

Step 3: Translate and Localize (Not Just Translate)

You don't want just translated content—you want localized experiences.

Localize for:

- Currency and pricing
- Date and time formats
- Measurements (cm vs inches)
- Language nuances, slang, tone
- Cultural references and examples
- Payment and delivery options

Bonus:

Use localized keywords, not just translations. What works in the UK might flop in Canada. For example, Google understands that when you use 'analyse' instead of 'analyze', you are trying to reach a UK audience.

Step 4: Set Geo-Targeting in Google Search Console

If you're using subdirectories or subdomains:

- Go to Search Console > Settings > International Targeting
- Set each subdomain/subfolder to its intended country

For ccTLDs (like .fr, .de)—Google already knows the country.

Step 5: Keep Internal Linking and Navigation Clean

- Use a language switcher that links to equivalent pages (not just homepages)
- Make sure your includes correct hreflang
- Don't block alternate versions via robots.txt

Mini Exercise: Quick International SEO Audit

1. Visit each language/country version of your site

   → Do they all link to one another properly?

2. View page source → search for hreflang

   → Are the correct tags in place?

3. Check your URLs: → Are you using subfolders, subdomains, or ccTLDs? Are they consistent?

4. Run your domain through Merkle's hreflang checker

Checklist: International SEO Done Right

- Proper domain structure in place (ccTLD / subfolder / subdomain)
- Hreflang tags on all relevant pages
- Google Search Console country targeting set
- Translations are localized (not literal)
- Internal links point to correct language/country versions
- Language switcher links page-to-page
- Site isn't serving the wrong version by IP redirect
- Localized keywords and content used for each region

Recap: Expand Without Breaking SEO

- Choose the right structure based on resources and goals
- Use hreflang to avoid duplicate content and language mix-ups
- Localize everything—from pricing to slang

- Be intentional, clear, and consistent across versions

Coming Up Next:

Let's get analytical. Chapter 18 is all about SEO Analytics and Reporting—because great SEO isn't just about doing, it's about tracking, proving, and improving.

Chapter 18: SEO Analytics and Reporting – Turn Data Into Strategy

If you're not tracking it, you're guessing. And guessing doesn't scale.

You can't improve what you don't measure.

SEO isn't just about optimizing pages, writing content, or building links—it's also about tracking progress, identifying what's working, and pivoting when things aren't.

This chapter is all about the metrics, tools, and frameworks you need to confidently analyze performance, communicate results, and make smarter SEO decisions.

The 3 Roles of SEO Analytics

1. Performance Tracking – Are your efforts actually working?
2. Issue Detection – What's broken, slipping, or underperforming?
3. Strategy Planning – Where should you focus next?

Great SEO reporting isn't just rows of numbers—it's insight + direction.

Core SEO Metrics to Track

Let's split them into categories:

1. **Organic Visibility**

- Impressions (Search Console): how often your pages show up in search
- Average Position: where your page appears on Google
- Keyword Rankings (tracked via tools like Ahrefs/Semrush)

2. **Traffic**

- Organic Sessions (Google Analytics): how many users came from search
- Landing Pages: which pages brought users in
- New vs Returning Users

3. **Engagement**

- Time on Page
- Bounce Rate
- Pages per Session

- Scroll Depth (in GA4 or Hotjar)

4. **Conversions**

- Form fills
- Product purchases
- Email signups
- Phone calls (tracked via call tracking tools)

Always tie SEO to business outcomes, not just rankings.

 If your client's traffic doubled but sales stayed flat, the SEO worked, but website needs additional work.

Tools You'll Want in Your Stack

You don't need all of these, but the more you grow, the more useful they become:

- Google Search Console – impressions, rankings, crawl errors, Core Web Vitals

- Google Analytics (GA4) – traffic, behavior, conversions
- Ahrefs/Semrush – keyword rankings, competitor tracking, backlinks
- Google Looker Studio – custom visual dashboards
- Screaming Frog / Sitebulb – technical SEO audits
- Hotjar / Microsoft Clarity – heatmaps, scroll maps, session recordings
- Rank tracking tools – SERPWatcher, AccuRanker, SEOmonitor

Creating Actionable SEO Reports

A good SEO report doesn't just say *what happened*. It answers:

- What changed?
- Why did it change?
- What are we doing about it?

Structure:

1. Summary of Key Wins/Losses
2. Organic Performance Overview
3. Keyword Movement
4. Top Pages
5. Technical Updates

6. Content Published or Optimized
7. Next Month's Priorities

Use visuals. Use plain English. Don't overwhelm. Highlight impact.

Reporting for Different Audiences

- Clients/Stakeholders → focus on business impact: traffic, leads, sales
- Internal SEO teams → show keyword movement, technical fixes, link progress
- Wider marketing teams → include cross-channel context and synergy

Tailor your message to what matters most to each group.

Mini Exercise: Build a 1-Page SEO Dashboard

Use Looker Studio or a spreadsheet to create a simple monthly snapshot:

- Organic traffic (past 30 days vs previous 30)
- Top 5 pages by traffic

- Top 10 keyword rankings (tracked manually or with Semrush)
- Conversions from organic
- New links earned
- Planned optimizations for next month

Keep it clean, skimmable, and focused.

Checklist: Analytics and Reporting Ready

- Google Search Console and GA4 installed and verified
- Keyword tracking tool connected
- Conversion goals set up (forms, eComm, calls)
- Monthly reports sent (internal or client-facing)
- Changes are tracked and tied to outcomes
- Insights are used to guide next month's strategy
- Dashboards exist for real-time tracking
- Clear definitions for KPIs (no vanity metrics)

Recap: Numbers Without Context Are Just Noise

- Track traffic, rankings, and conversions
- Build reports around actions, not just data
- Tie SEO wins to business goals

- Communicate clearly to stakeholders
- Use data to evolve your strategy, not just validate it

Coming Up Next:

We're entering the final section: Putting It All Together, where we'll show how to build and execute a long-term SEO strategy, troubleshoot common issues, and prepare for the future.

Chapter 19: Creating an SEO Strategy from Scratch – Your Step-by-Step Blueprint

SEO isn't a checklist—it's a system. And now you're going to build one.

At this point, you know how SEO works. You understand how to optimize content, structure your site, build authority, and track results.

But without a strategy, it's just a bunch of disconnected tasks.

This chapter walks you through building a real, long-term SEO strategy from the ground up—whether you're starting fresh or refining an existing site.

What Is an SEO Strategy (and What It Isn't)?

An SEO strategy is a focused plan that outlines how your content, technical setup, and promotional efforts will help you reach specific goals—traffic, leads, sales, or visibility.

What it's not:

- A random to-do list of SEO tasks

- An excuse to chase keywords without context
- A one-time setup (this is ongoing)

A strong strategy connects every action back to a purpose and a metric.

Step 1: Define Clear, Measurable Goals

What do you want to achieve with SEO?

- More traffic?
- Higher conversion rates?
- More visibility for your brand?
- Local customers? Global reach?

Be specific.

Bad: "I want more traffic"
Better: "I want to increase organic leads from product pages by 30% in the next 6 months"

Then decide on your key metrics:

- Organic traffic
- Keyword rankings
- Conversion rate
- Number of leads/sales
- Backlink growth

- Click-through rate (CTR)

Step 2: Know Your Audience and Their Intent

Everything starts with the searcher.

- Who are they?
- What are they struggling with?
- What questions are they asking?
- What kind of content are they searching for?

Segment your audience by:

- Stage in the buying journey (awareness, consideration, decision)
- Intent (informational, transactional, navigational)

Your keywords and content should reflect this.

Step 3: Build Your Keyword Strategy

Start with your core topics, then expand with tools like:

- Google Search Console (for existing opportunities)
- Semrush / Ahrefs (for keyword ideas and gaps)
- "People Also Ask" and related searches

- Competitor analysis

Group your keywords into themes:

- Product or service pages
- Blog clusters
- FAQs
- Local landing pages

Then prioritize based on:

- Search volume
- Intent match
- Ranking difficulty
- Relevance to your offering

Step 4: Set Up Your Site for SEO Success

Before publishing content, fix the basics:

- Crawlable, indexable structure
- Mobile optimization
- Fast load speed
- Proper meta tags and headings
- Schema markup where appropriate
- Sitemap and robots.txt configured
- Internal links in place

This is your technical foundation—without it, content won't rank.

Step 5: Create and Optimize Content

Now, build the right pages around your keyword plan.

- Homepage: strong positioning and keyword targeting
- Category/Product pages: optimized with unique copy
- Blog: pillar + cluster model
- Location pages (if local): city-specific content
- FAQs, About, Contact: complete and schema-ready

Use on-page SEO best practices:

- Optimized title tags and descriptions
- Clear headings (H1–H3)
- Image alt text
- Internal links
- Structured content for featured snippets

Step 6: Promote and Build Authority

Even great content needs help to get noticed.

- Promote via social media

- Build backlinks through outreach, guest posts, PR
- Use linkable assets (infographics, tools, studies)
- Repurpose blog posts into other formats (videos, carousels)

Set a consistent link building and promotion cadence—monthly or quarterly.

Step 7: Track, Adjust, and Repeat

SEO isn't "set and forget."

Monitor:

- Rankings (for core and secondary keywords)
- Traffic and behavior
- Conversions
- Backlink growth
- Technical health (crawl errors, speed, index status)

Then adjust your:

- Content (refresh or expand)
- Internal linking
- Keyword targeting
- Link acquisition focus

Sample Strategy Framework

Here's how a 6-month SEO strategy might look:

Month	Focus Area	Key Tasks	Due Date	Notes
Month 1	Audit & Research	- Technical SEO audit - Keyword research - Competitor gap analysis		
Month 2	Site Optimization	- Fix speed & mobile issues - Add schema to key pages - Internal linking update		
Month 3	Content Creation	- Write 3 blog posts - Build 1 pillar page - Launch FAQ section		Focus on high-intent keywords

Month 4	Link Building & PR	- Outreach to 10 blogs - Guest post 2 articles - Submit to directories		
Month 5	Expansion & Refresh	- Update old content - Launch 2 new landing pages - Add local pages		
Month 6	Analytics & Review	- Check rankings & traffic - Evaluate content ROI - Plan next cycle		Use Search Console & GA4

Mini Exercise: Draft Your 3-Month Plan

1. Write down 1–2 main SEO goals (traffic, sales, leads, etc.)
2. Choose 3 focus areas (e.g., blog content, product pages, technical fixes)
3. Assign 2–3 tasks per month
4. Schedule your first monthly review now

Checklist: Strategy Foundation Complete

- Goals defined and tied to metrics
- Audience and intent mapped
- Keyword research complete
- Site technically optimized
- Core pages and content structured
- Promotion plan in place
- Reporting systems active
- Review + improvement process scheduled

Recap: SEO Strategy = Consistency + Clarity

- Build a roadmap, not a task list

- Know what you're aiming for (and how to measure it)
- Don't chase hacks—build long-term assets
- Plan, do, measure, repeat

Coming Up Next:

Let's troubleshoot the bumps in the road. In Chapter 20, we'll cover Common SEO Problems—what causes them, how to fix them, and how to stay ahead of them before they tank your results.

Chapter 20: Troubleshooting Common SEO Problems – Diagnose, Fix, Recover

When something breaks, the right response makes all the difference.

SEO isn't static. Algorithms change. Sites break. Competitors level up. You might be doing everything right... and still lose traffic.

The key is knowing how to read the signals, find the cause, and respond with the right solution.

This chapter is your SEO emergency kit.

Problem 1: Sudden Drop in Rankings or Traffic

Possible Causes:

- Google Algorithm Update (check Search Console + industry chatter)
- Technical Error (deindexing, robots.txt, canonical issues)

- Site Structure Change (URL updates, broken redirects)
- Content Removed or Rewritten (losing keyword relevance)
- Manual Penalty (rare, but serious)

What to Check:

- Google Search Console → "Pages" and "Manual Actions"
- GA4 → sudden drop in organic sessions?
- Search your brand/site name—do you still appear?
- Use a tool like Semrush or Ahrefs to check keyword drops

Fix:

- Confirm it's not seasonal or external (like Google update)
- If technical: restore noindex'd pages, fix redirects, check schema
- If content-related: refresh pages, improve E-E-A-T, check intent
- If penalized: remove/fix offending links or spam, submit reconsideration

Problem 2: Pages Not Indexing

Possible Causes:

- Pages blocked by robots.txt or marked noindex
- Duplicate or thin content
- Crawl budget wasted (filters, tag pages, faceted navigation)
- Canonical tags pointing elsewhere

What to Check:

- Inspect URL in Search Console
- Use site:yourdomain.com/page-name in Google
- Look for robots/meta tags or canonical issues in HTML

Fix:

- Ensure important pages are crawlable and indexable
- Remove duplicate URLs and canonicalize
- Add internal links to orphan pages
- Submit sitemap and request indexing

Problem 3: Keyword Cannibalization

What is it?

Multiple pages on your site compete for the same keyword, confusing Google.

Symptoms:

- Ranking fluctuations
- Google switches which page ranks
- Neither page ranks well

Fix:

- Combine similar pages into one stronger page
- Use canonical tags or redirects
- Adjust targeting: assign separate, specific keywords to each page

Problem 4: High Traffic, Low Conversions

Possible Causes:

- Mismatch between traffic intent and page content
- Slow page, bad mobile UX

- Weak CTAs, unclear offer
- No trust signals (reviews, contact info, security)

What to Do:

- Revisit the page's intent vs. keyword
- Improve layout and UX
- Strengthen CTA and value proposition
- Add testimonials, trust badges, guarantees

Problem 5: Good Rankings, Low Click-Through Rate

Cause:

- Your snippet isn't compelling enough
- Meta title and description don't match intent
- Competitors have more enticing listings (e.g. stars, offers, structured markup)

Fix:

- Rewrite meta title and description to focus on benefits, clarity, and emotion
- Add schema (FAQ, Product, Review) to stand out
- Use brackets, numbers, or power words
- Test and improve based on CTR reports in GSC

Problem 6: Duplicate or Thin Content

What It Causes:

- Cannibalization
- Low-quality signal to Google
- Index bloat

Fix:

- Use canonical tags
- Noindex weak/duplicate pages
- Consolidate or rewrite content
- Add value: unique insight, visuals, original research

Problem 7: Lost or Toxic Backlinks

Symptoms:

- Drop in referring domains
- Traffic loss with no on-site changes
- Manual penalty notice (worst case)

What to Do:

- Use Ahrefs or Semrush to analyze link loss

- Reach out to reclaim broken links
- Disavow toxic links (only if you're confident and experienced)
- Focus on earning new, quality links

Mini Exercise: SEO Diagnosis Drill

Pick a problem (e.g. traffic drop, low CTR).

1. Use Google Search Console and GA4 to identify where it's happening
2. Run a crawl with Screaming Frog or Sitebulb
3. Check site: searches and competitor rankings
4. Document your findings
5. Create a short action plan: what to fix first, what to monitor

Troubleshooting Checklist

- Search Console shows no crawl/index issues
- Pages are not accidentally noindexed or canonicalized away
- No traffic or ranking drops from untracked changes
- Meta titles and descriptions are compelling and intent-aligned

- Pages are loading fast and work well on mobile
- Internal linking supports key pages
- You've checked for algorithm update impact
- No toxic backlink spikes or losses gone unnoticed

Recap: Don't Panic—Prioritize and Fix

- SEO problems are inevitable, but recoverable
- Most drops come from content decay, tech issues, or missed intent
- Diagnose methodically, fix fast, and track impact
- SEO is resilient—if you keep improving, growth will follow

Coming Up Next:
Chapter 21: The Future of SEO – Staying Ahead of the Curve. Because this isn't just about ranking today. It's about preparing for what's coming next.

Chapter 21: The Future of SEO – Staying Ahead of the Curve

Because SEO is never really finished—and that's the point.

SEO in 2010? Stuff some keywords, get backlinks, watch your site rise.
SEO in 2025? Compete with AI content, video-first SERPs, zero-click results, and a constantly evolving algorithm that mimics human behavior more than ever.

But here's the good news: the core principle hasn't changed.

If you create the best experience for the user, Google will reward you.

This final chapter is your compass for where SEO is headed—and how to stay relevant in a world where everything changes except the user's need for a great answer.

Trend 1: AI-Generated Content (and Google's Growing Skepticism)

AI writing tools have exploded—but mass AI content without originality will be penalized.

Google's *Helpful Content System* specifically targets:

- Unoriginal content
- Rewrites of existing info
- Pages made to rank—not to help

To stay ahead:

- Add personal experience, insights, or unique angles
- Focus on first-hand expertise (E-E-A-T)
- Include original images, video, data, or tools
- If you use AI—edit heavily, add depth, make it truly useful

Trend 2: The Rise of Zero-Click Searches

More and more searches end without a click:

- Featured snippets
- People Also Ask
- Maps
- Instant answers
- AI overviews (Search Generative Experience)

That's not a bug—it's the new SERP.

Your goal now:

- Be visible, even if the user doesn't click

- Own snippets, appear in "People Also Ask," and optimize titles for fast recognition
- Create *brand recognition*, not just rankings

```
If they don't click today but remember
your brand tomorrow—you still won.
```

Trend 3: Search Engines as Answer Engines

Google is no longer just a list of links—it's a decision assistant.

To win:

- Structure content clearly for AI and humans
- Add schema everywhere possible
- Anticipate and answer layered questions (FAQs, "what happens if," pros/cons)
- Include visuals, tables, comparisons

The better your formatting and clarity, the more likely your content becomes source material for future search results.

Trend 4: Multiformat Content Will Outrank Text-Only Sites

In 2025+, pages with rich media outperform plain text:

- Videos
- Carousels
- Interactive tools
- Audio snippets
- Charts and infographics

Start creating:

- Video summaries for blog posts
- Custom visuals to break down complex topics
- Tools or quizzes that engage

Google tracks engagement—not just words.

Trend 5: UX + Core Web Vitals = Ranking Factors That Stick

Speed. Stability. Interactivity.
 Google is watching it all.

Keep optimizing:

- CLS (Cumulative Layout Shift): avoid elements that move around
- LCP (Largest Contentful Paint): speed up loading of images
- INP (Interaction to Next Paint): reduce delay between click and response

Tools to use:

- PageSpeed Insights
- Web.dev
- Lighthouse (built into Chrome)

Trend 6: The Return of Authoritativeness

Google is leaning hard into:

- Real authors with real credentials
- First-hand experience
- Business trust signals (contact info, policies, location, brand mentions)

Your site should scream: *This is written by someone who knows what they're talking about.*

Add:

- Author bios
- Cited references
- Linked credentials
- Business verification (Local schema, Google Business, About pages)

Trend 7: SEO as a Career Asset (Not Just a Tactic)

SEO is no longer just a "marketing channel."
It's a core digital skillset:

- Freelancers use it to build personal brands
- Founders use it to reduce ad spend
- Creators use it to build discoverable content
- Companies rely on it for long-term growth

If you understand how search works, you control the attention pipeline. That's power.

Mini Exercise: Futureproof Scorecard

Rate yourself 1–5 on the following:

- My content reflects personal experience, not just summaries
- I use visuals, video, or tools in key content
- My site is technically fast and mobile-first
- I appear in snippets, FAQs, or People Also Ask
- I've claimed and optimized my Google Business Profile
- My authorship is real, visible, and credible
- I track what's changing in SEO monthly
- I write for users *first*, then optimize for search

<20? You're behind.
21–30? You're adapting.
31+? You're ahead of the curve.

Checklist: Staying Ahead in Modern SEO

- Use AI as an assistant, not a writer
- Optimize for visibility, not just clicks
- Structure content for readability + snippets
- Create content in multiple formats

- Improve UX continuously
- Establish authorship and credibility
- Follow SEO news via trusted sources
- Test, measure, improve—on repeat

Final Thoughts: SEO is About Mastery, Not Hacks

There's no magic trick to SEO.

If you've made it this far, you already know that. You've read about technical structure, user signals, content strategy, link-building, on-page optimization, and everything in between. But this book isn't just a checklist—it's a mindset shift.

I've written everything here from real, first-hand experience. These aren't theories copied from some blog or assumptions pulled from trends. Every technique, every tactic, every system I've shared with you has been tested—on real websites, under real client pressure, through Google updates, and across industries.

Some things worked.
Some failed miserably.
And others required months of tweaking, watching, re-testing, and rebuilding before they became part of my playbook.

This book is the distilled version of years of doing the actual work. I've had projects that ranked within weeks and others that took nearly a year to move from page three to page one. I've cleaned up backlink messes. Rebuilt bloated websites. Navigated client panic after algorithm drops. But through all of it, one thing became crystal clear:

SEO isn't about shortcuts. It's about earning your space—through clarity, structure, trust, and value.

You Don't Need to Be a "Guru"

The term *SEO expert* gets thrown around too easily. You don't need to be a guru. You need to be:

- Consistent
- Curious
- Open to feedback
- Focused on your audience

And above all, you need to be patient.

SEO is rarely instant. If you're chasing dopamine hits, go run ads. If you're building something to last, you're in the right game.

The Industry Will Keep Changing—Let It

Search will evolve.

Google will roll out another update.

Your favorite plugin will break after a theme update.

AI will reshape how we create, consume, and optimize content.

And you'll adapt.

Because great SEOs aren't obsessed with tricks. They're obsessed with making the internet better.

That's the mindset that never goes out of date.

My Parting Advice

Here's what I've learned (the hard way) that no Google doc or course tells you:

- Focus on people, not just systems
- Optimize for experience, not just rankings
- Use data, but listen to instinct
- Build authority slowly and ethically
- Stop looking for hacks—and start looking for momentum

Keep This Book Close—But Evolve Past It

You now have the frameworks, tools, and mental models I wish I had starting out. Use this book as a launchpad, not a finish line.

If there's one "hack" I'll admit to, it's this:

 Help more people, better than anyone else—and the rankings will follow.

Thanks for reading—and for building something that matters. Now go rank.